The road to the European Union

Albania and the Italian "partner"

Perparim Xhaferi

Marco Brunazzo

and Bruno Mascitelli

Connor Court Publishing

Copyright © 2022, Perparim Xhaferi, Marco Brunazzo and Bruno Mascitelli

ALL RIGHTS RESERVED. This book contains material protected under International and Federal Copyright Laws and Treaties. Any unauthorised reprint or use of this material is prohibited. No part of this book may be reproduced or transmitted in any form or by any means, electronic or mechanical, including photocopying, recording, or by any information storage and retrieval system without express written permission from the publisher.

CONNOR COURT PUBLISHING PTY LTD
PO Box 7257
Redland Bay QLD 4165
sales@connorcourt.com
www.connorcourt.com

Front cover picture: Post of Albania, Michel AL 3472 · Stamp Number AL 2962 · Yvert et Tellier AL 3143 · AFA number AL 3533, Wikipedia Commons, 2014.

ISBN: 9781922815279

Cover design by Maria Giordano

Printed in Australia

Other books by the authors

PERPARIM XHAFERI

ALBANIA: ESCAPING THE EAST, ASPIRING FOR THE WEST

MARCO BRUNAZZO

LA POLITICA DELL'UNIONE EUROPEA

ITALY IN THE EU: A ROLLERCOASTER JOURNEY

BRUNO MASCITELLI

ITALY AND AUSTRALIA: AN ASYMMETRICAL RELATIONSHIP with GIANFRANCO CRESCIANI

II GLOBO : FIFTY YEARS OF AN ITALIAN NEWSPAPER IN AUSTRALIA with SIMONE BATTISTON

Table of Contents

Acknowledgements   vii

About the Authors   ix

List of tables and figures   xi

1: The road to the European Union: Albania and the Italian "partner"   1

2: The Western Balkans: Escaping the Ottoman clutches amidst competing Italian interest   11

3: Albania and Italy: From the Great War to the end of World War Two   45

4: The Cold War: Albania's different path from Yugoslavia and Italy   71

5: Western Balkans move towards Europe – Italian interest in Albania subsides   103

6: The European Union and the accession of the Western Balkans   131

7: Western Balkans: In the "waiting room" for EU membership?   159

Bibliography   175

Index   185

Acknowledgements

We have a few circumstances and people to thank for helping this book to emerge as it has. Working under the shadow of Covid across the world and its restrictions has played a role in focusing our attention on this book. We like many others in the world relied on zoom to bring our thoughts together from across the globe. We are very thankful to Anthony Cappello, the publisher and his publishing company Connor Court for taking on this book on the basis of trust and little else. We are hopeful to have not let him down. Our thanks need to go to our respective families who have supported us through these times. This book is an outcome to say it was all worth it.

The authors, 31 August 2022

About the authors

Dr Perparim Xhaferi is a research fellow at the European Centre of excellence/RMIT University in Melbourne. He has been researching the European Integration focusing on the enlargement policy. His recent publications are *Albania: Escaping the East, Aspiring for the West,* (Brisbane, 2020) and "The Western Balkan Angst: Greater Albania" in *The European Union: New Leadership and New Agendas*, ed., Alomes, S., Park, S. C., and Mezyk, R., (Brisbane, 2021).

Marco Brunazzo is Professor of Political Science at the Department of Sociology and Social Research at the University of Trento (Italy). His main areas of interest are the EU differentiated integration theory, the role of Italy in the EU, and participatory democracy. Jean Monnet Chair in European Studies, between 2011 and 2016 he directed the Jean Monnet Centre of Excellence at the University of Trento. His most recent books are *La politica dell'Unione europea* (Milano, 2020) and *Italy in the EU: A Rollercoaster Journey* (New York, 2020).

Bruno Mascitelli is an Adjunct Professor at Swinburne University of Technology in Melbourne. He has taught in EU politics, researched and written extensively with a focus on European affairs and Italian political economy. He was a Jean Monnet Chair and he has published widely on Italian politics, expatriate voting and European studies.

List of tables and figures

Figure 2.1

Proposed boundaries at the London Conference 1913   38

Figure 3.1

Navigazione Adriatica – Albanian Lines 1937   56

Figure 3.2

Albania in 1939-1944   58

Table 4.1

Albanian trade with the West 1977 – 1984   88

Table 6.1

EU Enlargement of the Western Balkans: an overview   137

1

The road to the European Union: Albania and the Italian "partner"

For those who study the Western Balkans, it must rarely escape their attention that a regional location like the Western Balkans, with a population of circa 17.6 million, and with a combined gross domestic product (GDP) of around EUR 100 billion, can at the same time be the source of such human suffering and tragedy as it has been in the last century and more. Being no stranger to war, poverty, foreign invasions and ethnic cleansing, it is a subject which has been itself one with a large share of grief. The analysis contained in this book will inevitably tackle these experiences remembering there are always human beings behind these statistics, words and events.

This is a book about the interests, ambitions and geopolitical standing of Albania, Italy and the European Union and the association of their respective journeys through to their global positioning today. These three themes, at first sight, may not appear to be congruent either historically, politically, or culturally. Yet they are and our analysis will demonstrate that they not only share historical commonalities but that in today's geopolitical standing they also share future trajectories.

The journey provided in these pages focuses its attention on the 19th, 20th and 21st centuries and seeks to merge the Albanian journey to statehood through to the 21st century and its pursuit of joining the European Union. It also provides alongside Italy's rise as a new modern state in the 19th century through to its fascist phase in the early 20th century and then becoming a medium sized European power within the European Union. Finally, we address the rise of the European Union in the mid-20th century as a prospect for the future and its geopolitical collocation for European nations. Merging these three themes has been both a challenge but also an extraordinary revelation of a story entrenched and wound together in what appear to be separate pieces coming together like a completed painted canvas.

The Albanian journey detailed in this book describes its trajectory out of the shadows of the many hundred years of Ottoman control into modern statehood in the early twentieth century. But new statehood as we shall see, did not mean purpose and ability which would ensure its statehood and provide a clear political direction. It was a nation which was plundered politically and exploited and often unable to fend for itself. Always at odds with its neighbours, especially with Serbia and Greece, Albania's "independence" was overrun by another neighbour and rising regional middle power, Italy. Italy had shown special interest in its neighbour long before the invasion of the Fascist Mussolini government in 1939. While Italy's control of Albania was short-lived and overshadowed by the Second World War, it nonetheless exposed Italy's ongoing desire to see Albania as a part of its own.

While Albania and Yugoslavia ousted their previous corrupt governments in the middle of the twentieth century and replaced them with Socialist control along the lines of their counterparts in Eastern Europe, the rest of Western Europe would seek to reconstruct from the ruins of the Second World War. Emerging less than a decade after the end of the war was the ambitious genesis of a European project in the form of the 1951 Coal and Steel Authority. This was an attempt to respond to the never-ending warring of European nations, primarily Germany and France, and provide the first steps towards a Europe that would be more harmonious, cooperative and ambitious in its attempts to rebuild Europe. All of these developments were of course occurring under the shadow of a Cold War in Europe dividing East and West along ideological lines and imposing restrictive activities on both sides of this divide. From the late 1940s until the late 1980s this Cold War involving not only Eastern and Western Europe, but also the Western Balkans and especially Albania.

The Cold War in Europe came to an end between 1989 and 1991 with the Fall of the Berlin Wall, the collapse of Eastern Europe and the Soviet Union, producing a political earthquake of historic proportions throughout Europe and the world. Largely as a result of this, Yugoslavia and Albania simultaneously disintegrated producing separate independent states within the Western Balkans in more chaotic and violent episodes. The reverberations of the collapse of the Soviet Union in 1991 and its security consequences, are not limited to that period. The Russian invasion of Ukraine in early 2022 and its consequences on Europe and the European Union are in some respects unfinished business which also have a place in this book as will be demonstrated.

Some terminological clarity

There is no universal agreement on some territorial terms relevant to the themes of this book. Common understanding of the Balkans as an area includes Albania, Bosnia and Herzegovina, Bulgaria, Croatia, Greece, Kosovo, Montenegro, (now) North Macedonia, Romania, Serbia, and Slovenia. When it comes to the use of the Western Balkans, the list of countries only includes Albania, Serbia, Croatia, Montenegro, Bosnia and Herzegovina, North Macedonia and Kosovo. Throughout this book the term Western Balkans is prevalent and of course it is worth appreciating that there is also the area of the Eastern Balkans namely Bulgaria and Romania. Not often used as a geographical reference point as opposed to the Western Balkans.

The standouts in this list of Western Balkan countries include North Macedonia which only recently resolved its naming dispute with Greece in 2018 (known as the Prespa Agreement) opting for the name of North Macedonia as opposed to its provisional name after the collapse of Yugoslavia of the Former Yugoslav Republic of Macedonia (FYROM). Under the Yugoslav Socialist Federation, it was known simply as Macedonia and as it was in a different political world, objections to its name from Greece fell on deaf ears. This changed after the fall of Yugoslavia and the quest for Macedonian independence. The other standout is of course Kosovo. This region largely inhabited by Albanians has been at the centre of tensions between Albanians and Serbs for centuries. Brought to the fore of international attention with a war conducted by Serbia, ultimately resulting in NATO bombing of Belgrade in 1999, Kosovo as a separate independent state, is not recognised as such importantly by a number of European nations which will have some bearing on the story being told in this book.

Why a book on Albanian geopolitical trajectory towards the EU?

Our research has uncovered many aspects of this relationship – Albania – Italy – and the European Union which are insufficiently treated by the serious literature available. While a superficial understanding of Albania is available in more recent periods, the scholarly literature on Albania covering the last century is less than satisfactory. As such this study seeks to make a difference and what makes this book unique is the team of two Italian scholars who have researched extensively in Italian affairs and EU, complemented by the presence of an Albanian scholar who has lived and researched the Albanian literature in greater depth and unearthed numerous new developments which placed together allow for a new and original perspective on the Albanian political trajectory.

While we acknowledge the in-depth analysis of the Western Balkans by a small handful of social scientists, we are less glowing about the scholarly understanding of Albanian perspectives and political alternatives facing them. In many respects the literature on Albania demonstrates that stereotypes still portray Albania as an exotic and unknown country. Moreover, the majority of works of those Albanian writers who came after Enver Hoxha, such as the writings of Ismail Kadare, have reached the English reader through French translations only.

The Italian interest in this book also has a point and an objective. Given Italy's poor attempts historically to disassociate itself from its colonial aspirations of the past and possibly blaming fascist ventures for these colonial ambitions, there is an attempt in Italy post 1945 to see itself as separate from these ventures including that against Albania. The case of Albania is still viewed as a helpless situation where Italian aid for a poor neighbour overwhelms the national narrative. As was seen in different moments and especially in 1997, friendship quickly turned to hostility as thousands of desperate Albanians tried to enter Italy. Italian interests in Albania are more than a century old, predating fascism as Italy sought to overcome its limited territorial confines by seeking other shores. This study seeks to flush out Italy's interests and its overall approach towards Albania above and beyond what the rhetoric might be.

Finally, there is the presence of the ever-imposing European Union (despite Brexit) and the appeal of nations not yet members of it to be a part of this major conglomeration of countries. Albania joined NATO and has applied for EU membership. It is one of the Western Balkan nations undergoing an EU entry criteria process before being accepted for membership. But like other countries in the Western Balkan, and elsewhere, the ideals of getting "free lunches" from the EU need to be tempered with the fact that nations give more than they get from membership, especially those that might not be economically strong and have poor judicial, infrastructure and democratic legacies – like Albania.

Albania is also a country which has a bigger diaspora in numbers than those who live in the country. With a population of just over three million it can claim to a diaspora of a much bigger size. Its diaspora is both part of the making of the Western Balkans including large numbers in Kosovo, North Macedonia and Greece. There are also lesser numbers in other nearby countries. Given its poverty, Albanians have continued to trek across borders seeking opportunities elsewhere and also have significant diasporas in Europe and faraway continents including North and South America, Australia and elsewhere. Large diasporas of a country is never a good sign for the standing of a nation as it usually means the country was unable to cater for its burgeoning population which was forced to leave.

The modern context of Albania as an "independent" state in the 20th and 21st century

The Balkans and especially the Western Balkans were quite late in liberating themselves from the foreign occupiers like the Ottomans and others. By the time of "independence", the late 19th and early 20th centuries most of their Western and Eastern neighbours were well established as nation states. The Balkan Wars of 1912-13 provided extra resources for some of the Balkan nations like Serbia, and in 1912 Albania acquired its own independence from the Ottoman Empire. But Albania would be victim of territorial exploits from stronger neighbours and more importantly would be the pawn of Western powers designs in the region. These developments would then be subsumed by the encroaching Great War, triggered in July 1914 by the assassination of the Austrian Archduke Franz Ferdinand by the Bosnian Serb nationalist Gavrilo Princip. The Great War lasted four years and ended in November 1918. It left some 20 million dead soldiers and involved the competing global alliances concentrated around Austria-Hungary, Germany, the Ottoman Empire and

Bulgaria against the Allied Powers, Russia, France, Great Britain and later joined by Italy and the United States. The end of the Great War saw in Albania a short-lived monarchical state known as the Principality of Albania (1914–1925) followed by an even shorter-lived first Albanian Republic (1925–1928). Between 1928 and 1939 Albania was a Monarchy, ruled by King Zog I. A curious figure in Albanian history and this new kingdom would be supported by the Italian fascist regime until Italy's invasion and occupation of Albania in April 1939 an occupation which ended with the collapse of the fascist regime in 1943 and ended Italy's role as an Axis power.

After Germany invaded Yugoslavia in 1941, Yugoslav communists aided the establishment of the Albanian Communist Party (afterwards called the Party of Labour). Enver Hoxha became its leader and in 1944 the new Communist resistance was the only credible force remaining in Albania. While Albania was not part of the Yugoslav Federation, after 1944 it was administered and constructed along similar "Socialist" lines until its collapse in the early 1990s. Hoxha became Albania's Prime Minister from its liberation and remained its undisputed leader until his death in 1985. In 1948 he broke relations with Yugoslavia and formed an alliance with the Soviet Union. When Joseph Stalin died in 1953, Albania's relations with Stalin's successor, Nikita Khrushchev, deteriorated until Hoxha broke with him completely in 1961. He then forged ties with China which also turned sour soon after the death of Mao in 1978 and China's new warming of relations with the West. From 1978 until 1989 Albania entered a period of political and economic isolation from both East and West.

Hoxha's government used "Stalinist" methods of tolerating little to no political opposition. Using Marxism-Leninism as ideology, Hoxha's propaganda tried to convince Albanian population on the benefits of socialism, which meant equal distribution of the wealth. Soon after he came to power, Hoxha confiscated all the farmland from wealthy landowners and merged it into collective farms that were supposed to create some level of self-sufficiency in food crops. This was not perceived by Western nations in any positive manner but a sign of the brutal effects of the Socialist government in power. Moreover, this experiment had its limits – trying to build socialism in poverty was doomed from the outset. Despite the damage created, the non-violation of Albania's borders by foreign powers had been achieved – something Albania had rarely experienced in its history. This all came to an end in 1990-91 with the less violent but no less chaotic collapse of Albania.

The story of this book is how the Albanian journey intersected with Italian aspirations of Albanian control. The story examines the collapse of Albania and the option of allying itself with the West. This would be facilitated through the neighbourhood European project in the European Union alongside its security needs through membership of NATO. Our chapters are dedicated to explaining our understanding of how Albania responded to its challenges and how these intersected Italian as well as European interests.

Closing remarks

While preparing the manuscript for this book, Russia invaded Ukraine in February 2022. These events along with other parallel developments, the energy crisis and economic recession are providing for an exceptionally uncertain world, and few would have predicted that we would have found ourselves in this situation. But the Ukraine situation poses more complex scenarios for the European Union. Under the Von der Leyen leadership, Ukraine is being groomed for early membership of the European Union "they are one of us". As is discussed in chapter six, readers will see that the question of enlargement of new members is much less acceptable to European citizens than it was in the past and in some quarters, there is even hostility to it. Not surprisingly this matter has emerged as a grievance for Western Balkan countries and not just Serbia, as a direct supporter of Russia. The candidate members in the Western Balkans have agonised over the reforms needed for membership before being approved for membership. While Ukraine's membership of the European Union has a long way to go, the disenchantment within the Western Balkans has already begun and may have unexpected repercussions.

Finally, we are certain that the readers will enjoy reading this serious analysis of the Albanian journey from the Ottomans, through vulnerable statehood, then a period of Socialist isolation and eventually into what we have today. Its search for geopolitical positioning is what determines its placement today and one of its options is with the European Union. Along this journey we trace the Italian interest and relationship until more recent times when the European Union emerges as a direction for Albania's future direction. As scholars we have ensured that all the significant developments have been addressed along this journey, we have as would be expected at the same time provided our own analysis and narrative which sometimes will touch a chord of controversy and not be to everybody's tastes. We do not expect all to agree with what we say in this book, but we feel it is important to hear what we say and leave it to the reader to draw their own conclusion. We are sure you will enjoy this read.

2

The Western Balkans: Escaping the Ottoman clutches amidst competing Italian interest

In their bid to achieve independent nation status, the Western Balkans would in the nineteenth century trigger the context for what would be a bloody beginning to the 20th century with the Great War in 1914. Rising nationalism and the creation of nation-states by three ethnic compositions of the Western Balkans – Serbia, Greece and Albania will be at the centre of this chapter. Italy itself, an emerging new European power in the late 19th century and only recently liberated from the grasp of foreign powers, demonstrated its interest in the Western Balkans given its neighbouring proximity with special attention to Albania.

After its unification in the 1860s, Italian interests in the pursuit of foreign influence began initially looking across to Africa. Given its closer proximity to the Western Balkans, it was always of interest, but in order to pursue this interest Italy had to contend with two immediate obstacles: competition from other European powers contending for the Balkans and secondly, the ongoing presence of the Ottoman Empire. Italian colonial expansionism became clearer after their defeat of the Ottomans over Libya in 1911-12. However, the Western Balkans with the two Balkan Wars and subsequent Great War in 1914 would not be easy for the taking and its quest for independence would come at a high price.

The historic journey towards an independent Western Balkans

Since the fourteenth century, most of Western Balkan territories were under Ottoman occupation including today's Greece, North Macedonia, Albania, Kosovo, Montenegro, Bosnia & Herzegovina and Serbia. It was not until the beginning of the nineteenth century that the Western Balkans embarked on the road to independent nationhood forcing the Ottoman Empire to withdraw and permitting Western Balkan independence. It would be Serbia, with significant support coming from Russia, which would be the first to make its bid against the Ottomans. The Serbian uprising against the Ottomans was followed by Greek Independence and eventually in the second half of the nineteenth century, Albania made its bid for autonomy from The Porte. By the end of the eighteenth century, the Albanian elites would come together to finally assert their independence and push back on foreign imperial hegemony. However, there was little agreement on how to achieve this goal. The rise of Slavic nationalism in alliance with Russia, further damaged Ottoman rule in rural areas where Timar reforms were ineffective. Throughout much of the Western Balkans the national, ethnic, religious and cultural expressions collided with Ottoman rule, making it inevitable that these national aspirations would eventually cohere into national identities which would reject Ottoman rule.

Serbian uprising at the beginning of the nineteenth century

Serbia – the largest ethnic group within the Western Balkan, aspired for a united Yugoslavia in the region where it had significant influence. The concept of Yugoslavia initially was in effect a Slavic fraternity. An example of this fraternity was the Serb commemoration of the battle of Kosovo of 1389. The paradox of this celebration is that the Balkan forces under King Lazar of Serbia lost to the Ottomans, and yet Serbia built its concept of a nation-state precisely around this battle.

Not until 1810 did the French Marshal Aguste Marmont unite (though short lived) the divided territories and bring them under Napoleon rule. Not long after the failure of Napoleon's Russian campaign in 1812, French control of the area ended, producing greater trust between both Croats and Serbs towards Russia. The resistance against the Ottomans was unified in 1817, creating the birth of the principality of Serbia. Although Croatians at the beginning of the nineteenth century took the lead in trying to cohere and larger South Slav population under the name of Illyrianism, politics of South Slav nations were more complex.

The situation in Serbian lands under the Ottoman occupation was different from that of Croatia, which had been influenced by the Austro-Hungarian and Habsburg rule. The leader of the Croatian "Greater Illyria" movement Ljudevit Gaj was convinced that creating a unified Slavic language would overcome differences between the Orthodox followers and Catholicism that had been forced onto these populations by external powers.

However, the tensions went beyond the differences of religion. Ilija Garasanin (1812-74) was the first Serbian to articulate Serbian national ideology through what is known as Necertanije or Greater Serbia. Garasanin advocated for a stronger Serbia that needed to resist partition between Austria and Russia once the Ottomans withdrew. Both Prince Aleksandar and Garasanin who were interested in Serbian supremacy, and less so in Illyrianism, decided to work close with Croat Bosnians. Although Garasanin was antagonistic toward Illyrianists, he kept close contact with their leaders such as Gaj and Ban Jelacic, the governor of Croatia who organised the resistance against Hungarians in 1848. Necertanie argued that Serbian expansion was held in check by the Ottomans. Therefore, Garasanin felt that after the fall of Ottoman control it would be easier to expand the new Serbian Empire in the Western Balkans

(Judah 2009: 58). Greater Serbia's efforts were to be concentrated on Bosnia, Herzegovina, Montenegro and North Albania to secure the long-held dream of Serbian access to the Adriatic Sea.

Serbia's "permanent" enemy, Austria, occupied Bosnia in 1878 and it was not until the Balkan Wars (1912-13) that the old Serbia would include Kosovo and Sandzak again. Therefore, Necertanie was the representative of the new nationalism in Serbia, along with its spiritual leader, Garasanin. Necertanie's Serb nationalism remained important during the process of nation building in the nineteenth and twentieth centuries, and it can be argued that remnants of this nationalism are still present in Serbia today.

1821: Greece embarks on the path of independence

The Greek uprising that began in March 1821 followed on the heels of the rebellion movement of Ali Pasha of Ioannina. After his success in campaigns against the Russians, the Albanian commander, Ali Pasha was appointed by the Sultan to lead one of the four Albanian vilayets. The wealthy pasha developed his army and supporters and soon challenged Ottoman power, aiming to create an independent province. The Sultan's reaction to bring down Ali Pasha was immediate. The Ottoman troops moved to Ioannina, creating a power vacuum in the southern Greek islands and Morea. Both Greeks and Albanians, as well as other populations, inhabitants of today's Greece, benefited from this moment and sparked their resistance against the Ottomans.

The contribution of the Arvanites-Albanians during the uprising of Greeks in 1821-1830 was significant (Misha 1999: 25). The uprising was triggered by an impulsive reaction of the Panariot Prince Alexander Ypsilantis, who recruited heavily thus expanding the resistance. Ali Pasha's assassination by the Sultan troops in 1822 was followed by the massacre of some 30,000 people in the island of Chios. The last episode triggered European attention and sympathy for the Greek cause especially from Britain and France. In 1825 Russia, agreed with Britain to bring an end to the hostilities between Greek insurgents and the Ottoman Turks. The naval battle of Pylos between Britain, France, and Russia on one side and the Ottomans and Egyptians on the other was easily won by the European powers, which arguably paved the way for Greek independence. Greek propaganda reminded all of the "Western" heroes who died in the revolution between the "Western old Greece" against the Eastern Ottoman imperial regime.

Alongside Greece's Independence another concept flourished: Megali Idea or the Greater Idea which meant Greece's right to extend its territory. Similar to Necertanie in Serbia, Megali idea is at the heart of Greek nationalism, playing a significant role in Greek strategic positioning ever since the War for Independence in 1821. Since then, Greece has expanded its territory several times and since the enactment of the Greek constitution of 1844, until the end of World War Two, all Greek governments have promoted the Megali Idea. As part of these claims, for example, the South of Albania (considered by Greece as "North Epirus") belongs to Greece. The Epirus is known through successful campaigns against the Romans led by Illyrian, Pirrhus (Myrdal and Kessle 1976: 52) who reigned over the Epirus lands from 297–272 BC. A well-known Greek writer Kostas Krystallis who was born in Epirus, reveals in his valuable work symbolic similarities of Greeks and Albanians – people with different religion, but one leader – Skenderbeg, the King of Epirus (Potts 2010: 237). It is argued that Megali idea is still alive in the hearts and minds of modern Greeks.

What was happening to the Albanian-ness?

It is sometimes claimed that Albanian nationalism emerged much later compared to its neighbours Serbia and Greece. At the same time, Albanian opposition to the Ottomans was often bloodier than other part of Western Balkans. The best concrete example is the resistance that Gjergj Kastrioti, known as Skenderbeg, or Lord Alexander, organised for a quarter of a century (Hodgkinson 1999: 74). Although the concept of the Albanian nation itself is postcolonial, the League of Lezhë, or Alessio (known in Albanian as Besëlidhja e Lezhës), which was led by Skenderbeg, was in effect the first national military union with Albanian political aims against the Ottoman empire. The secessionist movement under Skenderbeg provoked mistrust from The Porte, as did Ali Pasha's uprising at the beginning of the nineteenth century. Similar to the post Skenderbeg period, following the assassination of Ali Pasha in 1822, Ottoman mistrust of Albanians increased, punishing harshly those Albanians who continued to resist The Porte. The culmination of this distrust was shown in August 1830, when the Sultan sent the Ottoman general Reshid Pasha to Monastir where 1,000 Albanian beys (landowners) were invited to a military celebration against the Greek resistance. Reshid Pasha unleashed a killing spree against 500 beys (Zickel and Iwaskiw 1994: 15-16), wanting to tighten the control of The Porte against Albanian opposition. This strategy succeeded in forcing further conversions to Islam and in delaying Albanian resistance against The Porte, but it would not last. In the long term, this massacre paved the way for the beginning of the Albanian national movement.

At the same time both Greece and Serbia were themselves Christian countries that opposed the Muslim Ottomans while Albania was seen as a Muslim country. Albanians implemented strategies of resistance against the perceived invincible enemy, especially in an environment such as Western Balkans where their direct neighbours,

Greece and Serbia aimed not only to oppose the Muslim Ottoman but also divide Albanian lands between them.

So why did Albanian nationalism increase in the second half of the nineteenth century? Failed attempts at modernizing and reorganizing the Ottoman Empire coincided with a further weakening of The Porte after their defeat by Russia in the second half of the nineteenth century. The winning Russians forced the Ottomans to sign the Treaty of San Stefano in March 1878. With this Treaty, the Ottomans were forced to cede part of their Balkan territory to then be distributed between Bulgaria, Serbia, Montenegro and Greece. The deal concerned the division of the Albanian speaking lands. The Albanians, who were considered by the Empire as Turks, were late in proposing their independent nationhood compared to Greece and Serbia which by 1878 had their own entities recognized by the Great Powers and the Ottomans. Thus, it was difficult for the Albanian speaking people to oppose decisions made by others at their expense. Albanian fears of their lands being partitioned fuelled Albanian nationalism. Albania suffered again at the hands of more powerful nations. The Treaty of San Stefano "created a large independent Bulgarian state and enlarged Serbia and Montenegro" at the expense of the Ottomans. Nevertheless, none of the emerging Balkan states were happy with the new borders created by the Treaty of San Stefano, let alone Albanian speaking people who suffered from the plans of the Great Powers, the Porte and their neighbours.

Bismarck's proclamation in 1878 "that an Albanian nation did not exist" terrified Albanians, who had been taught by bitter experience not to trust Russia in their plans of how to end the Ottoman rule and "aggrandize" themselves with the territories of Macedonia, Epirus, Thrace and Albania (Psilos 2006: 41). At best, the danger of Russia encouraging Albania's neighbours, Serbia and Greece, to partition Albanian-speaking territories considered Ottoman domains at the time, was real. Albanians understood this danger too well once they realised "the beginning of the end of the Empire, at least in its European territories" (Wasti 2016: 938).

The Ottoman-Islamic polity: Conversions to Islam

The Turkish-nomadic-pastoralism was gradually transformed in the Ottoman-Islamic polity by using 'jihad against Christians' approach as one of the main pillars of their policies. The aim was to establish elements of Islamic culture in every aspect of life such as agriculture, education, arts, crafts, religion, commerce, which in short, would contribute to the entertainment, peace and security for the House of Osman (Vryonis 1969-1970: 263). As such the Islamic religion became one of the strongest pillars of the Ottoman Empire. The Ottomans introduced Islamic features into everyday life in the Balkans, regardless of their ethnic background, and thereby enjoying more privileges than Christians. However, the Albanian language was prohibited by The Porte for Muslim Albanians who were not considered a millet but registered as Turks and thus, could only learn Turkish, whereas Orthodox Albanians would only learn Greek.

It is said that Albanians converted to Islam, as it was easier for them to live as Muslims rather than Christians within the Ottoman Empire. There was certainly significant economic, political and psychological pressure to convert to Islam. Christian Albanians had little choice as the State imposed Sunni Islam laws that were based on the sharia framework which privileged Muslims and disadvantaged Christians. With the Ottomans having fully conquered Albania, the Timar system was enforced in Albania and within the Western Balkan lands. Under this system, the Sipahis and Janissary (jeniçeri) military corps were at the service of the Sultan. The Sipahis were the political and civil servant elite mainly composed of the upper class of Muslim Turks. On the other hand, the Jenissary corps were Sultan's elite guard and were formed from Christian youth who were unable to serve in high ranks of the empire. Christians were required periodically to provide one healthy male child to be converted to Islam and trained to join the elite military corps of Janissaries – a policy known as devşirme. Many young boys from Albanian Christian families such as Skenderbeg became fighters for the Sultan's elite guard. This system not only caused emotional but also economic hardship for Albanian families, thereby losing healthy young males who might have contributed to their families and community. As one observer noted:

> ...the disadvantages in human, ethnological, and economic terms were overwhelming and...the devşirme system...[was] also the most prevalent example of forced conversion in the years predating the seventeenth century (Sugar 1977: 58-59).

As an example of the religious discrimination it was known that Albanian non-Muslims were subject to heavier taxes, devşirme, lack of educational opportunities and socio-economic status. Converting to Islam was considered normal especially given the lack of economic opportunities and working in menial jobs, while the Albanian Muslims were offered senior administrative positions, as they were considered allies of The Porte that "protected them from the Slavonic and the Greek encroachment" (Vickers and Pettifer 1997: 97). So many Albanian-speaking people had little choice and were forced to side with the lesser of the two evils.

Albanian nationalism on the rise

At the beginning of the 19th century The Porte introduced Tanzimat reforms aiming to re-organise and modernise the Empire in order to avoid further weakening of the Empire. Failed attempts at saving the Ottoman Empire coincided with a further weakening of

The Porte largely as a result of its defeat in the war against Russia in 1877-1878. For months after the Treaty of San Stefano was signed, on the first of July 1878, Albanian chieftains representing four vilayets of Kosovo, Janina, Shkodër and Manastir convened the "League for the Defense of Rights of the Albanian Nation" (Jelavich and Jelavich 1977: 224), known as the Prizren League. Initially the Prizren League was able to secure support from the Ottomans, as it aimed to unite all Albanian territories under the sovereignty of the ruling Sultan. As a result, all requests of the League leaders were in line with The Porte. However, leaders of the Prizren League had differing opinions regarding whether they should continue to accept the rule of the Sultan in the Albanian-speaking lands. The conservative faction under the leadership of Abdyl Frashëri (1839-1892) required autonomy from The Porte. The lack of unity between Albanians, however, did not stop the Prizren League in carrying out Albanian military actions against Serbia and Montenegro. The Porte used the Prizren League to fight its enemies but after realizing its aim of secession from The Porte, the Sultan refused to grant the League's requests, and brutally crushed it in 1881. This act was enough for Albanians to consider the League as a symbol of Albanian's resistance against the Ottomans. The Prizren League became part of Albanian Rilindja writer's songs, poems and folklore, which are still included in Albanian schoolbook texts (Rredhi, ND: 133-38). This was also a call for Albanians to rally around Albanian nationalism which raised the question of an Albanian nation-state. The seeds of an Albanian entity had now been sown by a more consistent Albanian political nationalism.

The six Great Powers of the time realized the eminent danger that was emerging due to disagreements on partitioning the Balkan Peninsula and agreed to hold the Berlin Congress. The Congress started on 13 June and was later finalised in a Treaty on 13 July 1878. The Prussian Chancellor Otto von Bismarck who promised to be an honest broker, chaired the Congress. The aim of the Treaty was to resolve territorial disputes in the Balkans, but in reality, it further fractured already tense relationships and alliances in the region. The Congress began poorly for Albania who were not recognized as an ethnic entity. Moreover, reversing the recognition of Macedonia and including its territory within the larger Bulgaria, meant returning its territory to the Ottoman Empire. Bulgaria, Greece, Montenegro, and Serbia "perceived in the Treaty of Berlin a barrier to their national aspirations", therefore, after 1878, "all the Balkan states strove to overcome the Berlin settlement and realize national unity" (Hall 2000: 3). The frustration infuriated Albanian nationalists who were concerned with these developments.

The genesis of colonial aspirations before the creation of the Italian State

Colonial aspirations by Italy surprisingly appeared even before Italy became a unified state.

One observer noted:

> Although Italian colonialism was more restricted in geographical scope and duration than the French and British Empires, it had no less an impact on the development of metropolitan conceptions of race, national identity, and geopolitical imaginaries. Indeed, since Italy began acquiring protectorates (Aseb and Massawa) just a few years after unification in 1870, and since Italy's first national war was a colonial one (the Italo-Turkish War over Libya in 1911-1912, to could be argued that in Italy colonialism was even more central to the construction of nationhood... (Ben-Ghiat & Fuller, 2008: 1-2).

The occupation of Italy by Napoleon in the late 1700s and its actions in deposing Kings in many of the regional states, making life more difficult for landowners and the removal of the Pope from Rome inspired some within the population to rally around a united identity. This however was short lived when the fall of Napoleon in 1815 and the Congress of Vienna in the same year – saw Italy return to its usual divided order and the return of former rulers. An opportunity for Italian statehood was dashed yet again. Mazzini, one of the initial voices of Italian unification at the time made the apt and gloomy prediction for the prospects of Italian unity in the aftermath of the 1815 Congress saying:

> We have no flag, no political name, no rank among European nations. We have no common centre, no common fact, no common market. We are dismembered into eight states – Lombardy, Parma, Tuscany, Modena, Lucca and Popedom, Piedmont, the Kingdom of Naples – all independent of one another, without alliance, without unity of aim, without organised connection between them... Eight different systems of currency, weights and measures, civil, commercial and penal legislation, of administrative organisation and of police restriction, divide us and render us as much as possible strangers to each other (Mazzini taken from Leeds 1974: 12).

Some decades later Neapolitan historian Luigi Blanch provided context to this division within the yet to emerge Italian state stating:

> The patriotism of the Italians is like that of the ancient Greeks and is love of a single town, not a country; it is the feeling of a tribe, not a nation. Only by foreign conquest have they ever been united. Leave them to themselves and they split into fragments (Leeds: 1974:13).

Fragmented and localised resistance to the ruling authorities, after 1815 like the Carbonari, was evident and made up of articulate middle-class elites, lawyers, army officers and the like though they found it difficult to provide common cause throughout the country.

Silvio Pellico was a member of the Carbonari arrested in 1820 and spent 10 years in prison in Bohemia for a minor offence. His *Le Mie Prigioni* was a powerful testimony to the ideological desires of this movement and for a free and independent Italy. The Carbonari were much bigger than many realised at the time and in 1820 it was estimated to number around 300,000 supporters. As Leeds indicates, the Carbonari were the main oppositional influence until the 1830s, when this movement was overtaken by the Association of Young Italy (*La Giovina Italia*) formed by Giuseppe Mazzini (Leeds 1974). The new association which had a more radical agenda and one which sought Italian independence was by 1833 considered by the Austrian authorities, dangerous and declared that membership of this association would be punishable by death. Mazzini, initially imprisoned and from 1831 exiled, took the reins of this Young Italy expounding its views even if afar.

Austria was one of the major European powers and competed with Prussia for domination of Germany, which like Italy, was fragmented and divided into many states. While Austria was German speaking, its alliance with the Hungarians provided for a very differentiated empire. 80 per cent of the population of the empire were from various regions such as the Magyars, Czechs, Poles, Rumanians, Croats and Italians most of whom remained under Austrian rule until 1918.

Between 1845 and 1848 Italy along with other parts of Europe would witness massive social and political protest known as the Revolutions of 1848. Beginning in Paris in February when it overthrew the Constitutional Monarchy of Louis Philippe and rapidly progressed to Germany and then Austria crippling the Habsburg monarchy. In Italy the revolution saw a number of city revolts which eventually merged to become a national event. The armed insurrection in Milan produced the "5 days of Milan" (*Cinque giornate di Milano*) which occurred between 18-22 March 1848 in the then capital of the Lombardy-Venetian State bringing temporary liberation from the Austrian rulers. These revolts however were temporary and eventually each was subdued. The reasons for the failure were the same as always. It would be Piedmont under the jurisdiction of the House of Savoy with Cavour in the government which would provide the pretext for potential Italian unity by provoking Austria into war over Piedmont. In July 1859 France and Austria eventually signed an armistice. Even the locality of Sicily began revolting against their Bourbon rulers which attracted the concern and attention of Garibaldi. Unrelenting and failing to listen to his superiors, Garibaldi launched his One Thousand Volunteers to invade and take over Sicily from the Bourbons and place them with the Kingdom and Piedmont. Eventually in 1860 under the rule of the King he was able to declare: "Our country is no more the Italy of the Romans, nor the Italy of the Middle Ages; no longer the field of every foreign ambition, it becomes, henceforth, the Italy of the Italians" (Martinengo-Cesaresco, 1895, cited in Leeds 1974: 70). However, this conglomeration did not include the Papal States or the Venetian Region. This would require a further 10-year struggle concluded in 1870. Rome was now in the hands of an Italian unified independent state.

The establishment of the Italian unified state

The establishment of the Italian Unified State was a product of two different moments. In 1861 with the formal establishment of the Kingdom of Italy and almost a decade later in 1870 when inhabitants in Rome voted in a plebiscite to endorse a unitary State. According to some what shattered the old Italian statelets was the effects of the conquests of Napoleon in the 18th century. It was in effect Napoleon's invasions which destroyed the separate regional power elites. Kings and centuries old republics of Venice and Genoa were destroyed, and the pope was removed from Rome. Only the two islands of Sicily and Sardinia retained their independence. Prior to the establishment of the unified Italian State, Italy had been the playground for foreign forces. For hundreds of years Italian principalities separated by local power structures and at war with each other, foreign forces found local environments even supportive. Mack Smith noted:

> No foreign conqueror in Italy failed to find active support among the local population: this was true of the French in the 1490s, as of the Spanish in the 1280s, the Germans in the twelfth century, and the Arabs in the ninth. It was also true of Napoleon's invasions in 1796 and 1800 (Mack Smith 1968: 2).

Towards the end of the century, successive Italian governments began to focus on foreign ambitions, primarily towards Northern Africa and the Balkans - especially Albania. It is not the intent in this book to focus on Italy's African ventures except to note that it occupied many resources and thinking by Italian policy makers in their quest for "a new coastline". Like many imperial ventures, the initial groundwork was undertaken by religious pioneers as was the case with Italy when Catholic missionaries began their activities as early as 1837. Only a few years after the 1860 unification, Rubattino, an Italian shipping company purchased rights to the bay of Aseb in Eritrea which in only a little more than a decade would control the entire bay (Ben-Ghiat & Fuller 2008: xiv). This private initiative would be taken over by the Italian government in 1882, becoming modern Italy's first overseas territory.

The obstacle which Italy would face in terms of colonial ambitions was its difficulty in becoming a unified voice and state. In 1882 Italy joined the aspiring European powers of the Triple Alliance which included Germany and Austria. In 1887 when this Treaty was up for renewal, the Italian government sought to insert a clause that inferred that there could be territorial concessions to Austria-Hungary achieved territorial gains in the Balkans (Varsori 2012). Some years later, the annexation of Bosnia-Herzegovina by Austria-Hungary temporarily thwarted Italy's aspirations on the Balkans but the matter would not go away.

In the early 1890s Italy's diplomats in Turkey took greater interest in Albania including reinforcing cultural exchanges and seeking to "turn Albanians into Italians" (Batir 2012). This was undertaken through schools, scholarships and other Italian facilities. It included significant people exchanges through travel between Brindisi and Durrës. An active campaign by Italy heightening the tensions between Greece and Albania was in progress seeking to win over the Albanian hearts and minds with whatever it took.

Even before 1897 Italian interest in Albania had been bubbling with Prime Minister Crispi, himself with some Albanian ancestry, repeating the Italian interest in Albanian. In the standoff with Austro-Hungary there was the implied understanding that "good" relations between Rome and Vienna required Austro-Hungarian staying away from Albania. At the time Italy saw the importance of investing in Italian schools in Albania and of financially supporting the leading members of the Albanian Catholic clergy – an action which was overturned in 1896 (Wickham Steed 1927).

Now a unified nation-state, Italy intended to compete with the other European powers for the new age of European colonial expansion. Its interests lay in the Mediterranean and in the Horn of Africa, a region still unclaimed and with access to ports and waterways. With a large community of Tunisian Italians in the Ottoman Province of Tunisia, Italy had long considered this area to be within its economic sphere of influence. It moved on its annexation in 1879, when moves were afoot for France to add it to its colonial holdings in North Africa. French troops eventually entered Tunisia from French Algeria, imposing a protectorate over Tunisia in May 1881 under the Treaty of Bardo. This unexpected development forced an angry Italy to sense its isolation in Europe and eventually led it into signing the Triple Alliance in 1882 with Germany and Austria-Hungary.

In 1886 Italy's search for colonies continued and by secret

agreement with Britain, it annexed the port of Massawa in Eritrea on the Red Sea which would deny the Ethiopian Empire of Yohannes IV an outlet to the sea. At the same time, Italy occupied the south side of the horn of Africa in what would become Italian Somaliland. A year later Italian Prime Minister Depretis ordered the invasion of Ethiopia leading to the Eritrean War. The invasion was eventually halted after Italy recorded a loss of 500 troops at the Battle of Dogali. Francesco Crispi, who succeeded Depretis signed the Treaty of Wuchale in 1889 with Menelik II, as the new emperor. This treaty ceded Ethiopian territory around Massawa to Italy to form the colony of Italian Eritrea and made Ethiopia an Italian protectorate. Relations between Italy and Menelik deteriorated over the next few years leading to the outbreak of war in 1895. Poorly equipped and outnumbered, Italy suffered a decisive defeat at the hands of Ethiopian forces at the Battle of Adwa in 1896.

Young Turk revolution and the united Albanian front

The beginning of the 20th century found the Ottoman Empire on shaky ground. The unsuccessful Tanzimat reforms ended with the First Constitutional Era in 1876 and Russo-Turkish wars of 1877-1878 further jeopardised the economic and political situation of The Porte. At the beginning of the 20th century, a new political reform movement, the Young Turks, promoted the replacement of the Ottoman Empire's absolute monarchy with a constitutional government. In July 1908, one of the main factions of the Young Turk forces, the Committee of Union and Progress (CUP), challenged the Sultan and demanded the restitution of the 1876 constitution. Inspired by Western European movements, they requested the establishment of a parliamentary system which was to be formed from free elections, and the change of the state structure aiming to guarantee more ethnic unity "irrespective of nationality or religion" (Psilos 2006: 29). The Sultan, Abdul Hamid capitulated in July

1908 and a new constitution was restored. The Albanian leaders across Albanian speaking lands during the Parliamentary session in December 1908 supported the new constitution. The Young Turks promised democratic parliamentary reforms which would deliver "religious freedom, free education, freedom of the press, freedom of speech and assembly" in all Albanian speaking lands (Pearson 2004: 2). However, except for the freedom of the press, and despite all the promises none of the rights were conceded by the Young Turks. Frustrated with the Young Turks and conscious of the risk their neighbours professed, the Albanian political elite began to coalesce around their anti-Turkish movement, which in 1909, surged on multiple fronts. In addition to the Albanian military resistance throughout 1909-1910, their leaders put forward demands at the Manastir Congress, Tepelena convention, Dibër and Elbasan congress. In these deliberations they requested freedom of education in Albania, protection of the Albanian language, the Latin alphabet, Albanian culture and protection from the danger of Serbian and Hellenic expansionist programs (Psilos 2006: 31-37).

The Porte reacted promptly to this quasi Albanian insurrection. In April 1910, the Sultan decided to put a stop to this movement by sending his general, Turgut Pasha, who led a new military campaign aiming to restore order, collect overdue taxes, and disarm the Albanian tribes. The anti-Turkish campaign led by Isa Boletini and Idriz Seferi reached its peak when in spring 1910 when 3000 Albanian forces blocked the railway to Skopje at the Kaçanic Pass. The Ottomans were concerned when 16,000 Ottoman troops were unable to quell the small Albanian forces and needed to boost their forces to 40,000. They entered Shkodër in July 1910 burning villages forcing 150,000 people to leave their homes. The Ottoman campaign came to an end in October 1910, leaving Albania in total "devastation and anarchy" (Psilos 2006: 37). These developments prompted Albanian resistance in the North into organised armed resistance against The Porte in Spring 1911. The Ottomans concerned by these developments called on Albanian chieftains to agree to a cease-fire.

The uprising was further inflamed in April 1911 when an Italo-Albanian, Terenzio Tocci proclaimed the independence of Albania, raising the Albanian flag at the Mirëdita mountains. In June 1911, the leaders of the Albanian uprising from the assembly of Greçë in Montenegro presented their political demands to the Turkish Cabinet including territorial and administrative autonomy for all Albanian speaking lands, the recognition of the Albanian nationality with Albanian language rights, and a general amnesty be granted for all Albanians "…who have been sentenced for political reasons" (Pearson 2004: 18). Although the Sultan signed an amnesty in July 1911, sceptical Albanian insurgents refused to return home as their political requests had not been fulfilled. The Albanian Malissori chieftains re-organised Albanian forces and in August 1912, sent a memorandum to the Sultan with further fourteen demands, similar to that of Greçë (Pearson 2004: 26). Other Albanian leaders increased pressure from the South and captured the towns of Durrës, Krujë and Peshkopi in the vilayet of Shkodër, and Fier and Përmet in the vilayet of Janina. This increasing pressure forced the Sultan to cede to some of the Albanian demands but refused to recognise Albanian autonomy.

A united political platform of the Albanian national liberation, evolving into armed resistance, was now becoming a serious threat to The Porte but also Serbia and Greece. This state of play was well understood by the Serbian government that did not hesitate to use Serbian nationalism in attempting to hijack Albanian resistance. An example was the Albanian uprising of North Albania and Kosovo, which in autumn of 1912, was instigated by "a Serbian terrorist organisation"—the Black Hand Society. Its leader, Dragutin Dimitrijevic, promised help and encouraged Kosovar Albanians in their revolt against the Turks (Pearson 2004: 27). The aim of the Serb nationalists was to separate Turks from Albanians, and according to one observation "...the Serbs and Montenegrins [who] massacred them [Albanians] wholesale" (Pearson 2004: 28).

Atrocities by Serbs and Montenegrins against the Albanian population reinforced the point among Albanians that the Ottomans had failed to protect Albanians. Furthermore, anxiety for Albanians increased after the Balkan League agreement in the spring of 1912 when Bulgaria, Serbia and Greece inspired by Russia agreed to create the Orthodox brotherhood of "The Balkan League"; aiming to fight the Ottoman oppressors and drive Macedonian lands out of the Turkish dominion. Albanian leaders interpreted the Balkan League to be not only anti Turkish, but mostly anti-Albanian. It was clear that:

> ...none of the other Balkan States wished to see an independent Albania, but rather envisaged the partition of Albania between them. Thus, they hastened to precipitate war with Turkey, the purpose of which was the annexation of Albanian-inhabited territories that were under Turkish rule (Pearson 2004: 27).

Renewed interest in Albania – The Cretan Insurrection of 1897

The Cretan Insurrection between Turkey and Greece in 1897 brought the Balkans again to the foreground for the contending parties including the new Italian unitary state. Austria-Hungary and Russia were both seeking an agreement to apportion their areas of influence in the agreement signed in St Petersburg. The Western Balkans, including Albania, fell into the Austrian sphere. Soon after these events, the Italian Foreign Minister at the time, Visconti Venosta, sought a reassurance from Austria that both Austria and Italy would not take any action into Albania. These sentiments were reconfirmed on numerous occasions by both states in 1900, 1905 and again in 1906. Italy however was distrusting of the Austrians and continued to support schools and the Albanian clergy as well as some of the more influential chieftains (Wickham Steed 1927). Italian intentions rarely were espoused so clearly as when the Italian Minister for Foreign Affairs Tittoni in 1904 explained Italy's interest in Albania:

> Albania in itself is not of great importance. ...Its real value consists in its ports and its coasts, the possession of which for either Austria-Hungary or Italy would signify incontestable supremacy in the Adriatic (Capps,1963: 12).

A wave of nationalism swept Italy at the turn of the 20th century some of which proposed the expansion of Italy's sphere of influence. The Italian media spoke of revenge for the humiliations suffered in Ethiopia at the end of the previous century, and as often is done by nationalists, nostalgia for the Roman era. Ludicrous suggestions emerged that Libya, was an ex-Roman colony, which should be returned to Italy in order to provide a solution to the problems of Southern Italy's population growth. Concerned that Britain and France would exclude Italy from North Africa altogether and in line with sections of public opinion, Prime Minister Giolitti ordered the declaration of war on the Ottoman Empire in October 1911, of which Libya was part.

The Turkish-Italian war 1911-12

The Italo-Turkish War over Libya in 1911-12 was itself a military confrontation which had other geographic ramifications, including that of the Balkans. It was a war against Turkey to access the Turkish provinces of Tripolitana and Cyrenaica (today modern Libya) in Northern Africa. Taking advantage of international paralysis after the Moroccan crisis of 1911, Italy pursued its long-desired goal of establishing a colony in North Africa. With the excuse that Turkey had infringed Italian concerns in the two provinces, the Italian government issued an ultimatum to Turkey on September 28, 1911, and on the next day declared war. Italian forces quickly occupied the towns of Tripoli, Darnah (Derna), and Banghāzī (Benghazi), although resistance from the local population forced Italian forces to limit their operations to the coastal areas. In May 1912 Italian naval forces occupied Rhodes and some of the Dodecanese islands off the Turkish coast, but the war remained a stalemate until a successful Italian military offensive in North Africa between July and October 1912. Turkey, now menaced by the Balkan states, sought peace. By the terms of the Treaty of Lausanne (also called Treaty of Ouchy, October 18, 1912), Turkey conceded its rights over Tripoli and Cyrenaica to Italy. The conflict upset the precarious international balance of power just prior to World War One by revealing Turkey's weaknesses and equally within Italy, it unleashed a nationalist-expansionist sentiment that guided government policy in the following decades. The war was seen as a weakening of the Ottoman rule and therefore openings for independent nation states in the Balkans.

In the light of its colonial ambitions, the Italian government in 1912 constituted a Ministry of the Colonies. The Ministry was established to manage and direct its external territories now known as the Italian Colonial Empire which included the territories of present-day Libya, Somalia, Ethiopia and Eritrea. Outside Africa, Italy possessed the Dodecanese Islands and a concession in Tianjin in China (following the Boxer Rebellion). Even before the Italian invasion of Albania in 1939, Italy imposed protectorate status on Albania from 1917 to 1920 and from 1925 to 1939. There was little doubt that there was consistency in Italian desires for external territories between the pre fascist and fascist regime.

From Albanian independence to Balkan Wars

The first Balkan War that broke out in October 1912 directly threatened Albanian speaking lands. The following month, on 28 November 1912, Ismail Qemali and representatives from Albanian speaking lands, travelled to Vlorë and declared Albanian independence. This symbolic act ended the Ottoman occupation of Albanian territories, but the challenge of the recognition of the Albanian state remained. The immediate tasks for the Albanian leaders were to unite the Albanian army, reviving the Albanian depressed economy and its institutions, but most importantly, seek out recognition of the Albanian state by Great Powers.

In December 1912, the Balkan League convinced the Ottomans to sign a cease-fire. This created a further opportunity for the Balkan League armies of Serbia, Montenegro, Bulgaria and Greece to attack the Albanian lands. Turkish troops gradually started to withdraw from Albanian vilayets to mark the end of the Ottoman era in Albania, creating more anxiety among Albanian leaders who knew that Albania's neighbours were ready to advance and fill the vacuum left by the Ottomans. As one observation noted:

> Certainly, Bulgaria, Greece, Montenegro and Serbia showed not the slightest hesitation or moral qualm in planning the partition of Albanian lands (Jelavich and Jelavich 1977: 320).

The Austrian empire kept an eye on Serbia and once more the opportunity to consolidate the Albanian Adriatic exit was presented. Therefore, Serbian troops that were present in Macedonia moved quickly through via Egnatia and established control over the north bank of Shkumbin River in central Albania (Hall 2000: 85). Serbia was aiming to hold the north of the Shkumbin River, which would secure them both existing ports of Durrës and Shëngjin, thus, realizing Serbia's dream to have access to the Adriatic Sea.

Although the first Balkan War was brief and was not contained solely to Albania, it did however produce the clear danger of Albanian division by Serbia in North and Greece in the South. Greek forces surrounded the Ottoman troops of Esat Pasha on 14 December 1912 in what is known as the siege of Janina. A volunteer legion led by the son of the Italian national hero Giuseppe Garibaldi—Ricciotti Garibaldi soon reached Janina to unite with the Greeks. The siege lasted months and ended in March 1913, with an Ottoman defeat. The Greek troops quickly advanced North to penetrate Albanian lands and to secure the Ionian coast and Corfu, demonstrating an effective and agile military.

Serbia did not stop at the north bank of Shkumbin River, but in defeating the Ottomans they entered Lushnje and then Berat in Central Albania in March 1913 when they were forced to conclude their advancement in Albania. By the end of April, pressure from the Great Powers increased forcing Serbia to withdraw from Central and North Albania. By then, the Austro-Hungarian Army had already entered Bosnian lands and threatened King Nikola of Montenegro forcing him to surrender with the Great Powers assuming control, ultimately ending the First Balkan War. With the signing of the Peace Treaty in May 1913, the first Balkan War came to an end. This Treaty decided that Macedonian lands would be divided between Serbia and Greece, thus escalating Bulgarian nationalism. Turning its attention to Adrianople, and with the support of Austro-Hungary, in June 1913, Bulgaria attacked both Serbia and Greece, sparking the second Balkan War however it was not a difficult task for the armies of Serbia, Greece, Romania and Turkey to defeat Bulgaria in this Second Balkan War. The Treaty of Bucharest, which was agreed in August 1913, was negotiated without the presence of the Great Powers and marked the end of the second Balkan War. This Treaty recognised that Bulgaria would drop claims on the Macedonian lands, which were now to be divided between Serbia and Greece—both Balkan states that were still hoping on dividing Albanian territory. Russia's strong support for Serbian victories infuriated Austro-

Hungary and Germany as Russia became closer to an alliance with France and Britain. The Great Powers found themselves on multiple fronts in contrast with each other and as 1914 approached, ominous signs of tensions spilling over were becoming evident. It was of course the lead up to the outbreak of the bloody Great War.

The London Conference – and the destiny of "little" Albania, 1912-1913.

The ceasefire between the Ottoman-Turks and the Balkan League in 1913 forced the Great powers to act swiftly to minimise the potential danger that was approaching the Balkans. The aim was to find a diplomatic solution to the tensions caused by partitioning of the "Ottoman lands" in the Balkans. The London Conference, or what is known as the Ambassadors' meetings, was chaired by the British foreign minister Edward Grey, and officially opened on 17 December 1912, and continued to meet during both Balkan wars.

The status of Albania became a permanent feature on the agenda. The main Albanian supporters, Austria and Italy fought to bring Albania under their influence. The key event being proposed by Russia was Serbian access to the Adriatic Sea. Both Italy and Austria rejected this request. They both argued that Albania should exist as a neutral country and despite opposition from Serbia and Greece, the London conference accepted this approach.

A principality of Albania was established and Prince William of Wied, cousin of the German Emperor and related to the Dutch and Romanian dynasties, was appointed Prince. However historic tensions would not disappear. Hostile relations between Serbia and the Albanians remained owing to the incursions into Albanian territory and Serbian annoyance at the refusal of the Conference of Ambassadors to grant her access to the Adriatic. Another source of ongoing tension was the status of Greece in the North part of Epirus, provisionally included in Albania and constituting a source of difficulty between Greece, Albania, and the Great Powers. However, as the political aim of the Conference was to bring peace to Europe, The Ambassadors Conference assumed the task of re-drawing the ex-Ottoman territories in the Balkans, which simply meant rewarding Balkan winners with territories from the Ottoman four vilayets of Janina, Manastir, Kosovo and Shkodër.

The main events of the London Conference included the disputes between Austro-Hungary and Italy on one side and Russia and France on the other. Grey, who was supposed to represent the neutral position of the UK, in reality sought to protect British interests, especially when dealing with Greece. Grey had to bargain between positions of Austro-Hungary – known as a strong supporter of the Albanian case, and Russia – known for its historical support of the Slavs in the Balkans, especially Serbia. Three proposals were presented to Grey: one from Austro-Hungary and Italy, one from Russia and France and one from the Albanian delegation. The Russian proposal lobbied for Serbian, Montenegrin, Bulgarian and Greek interests at the expense of Albanian-speaking territories, primarily focused on the Serbian need for securing Adriatic Sea access. The proposal included within the Serbian territories the plains of Kosova and North Albania. The Russian strategy was clear: at the very least the port of Shëngjin needed to be secured for Serbia.

Unlike the Russian approach, the Austro-Hungarian proposal strongly lobbied for Shkodër, and with it Shëngjin to remain part of Albania. With their decision to deny Serbian access to the Adriatic Sea, Austro-Hungary's aim was twofold: inhibiting Serbian economic expansion and confining the Russian expansion in the Balkans. Austro-Hungary and Italy spent much of their energy to secure Shkodër for Albania and to block Serbian access to the Adriatic Sea while opposing Greece's claims on South Albania.

While the Ottoman delegation withdrew from the Conference,

the Albanian delegation composed of a Muslim, Mehmet Konica, a Catholic, Filip Noga, and Rasim Dino, who represented the Chameria (Çamëria) region, had 13 minutes to present their case. Konica claimed that Albanian territory should include all parts of Albania shown in the Austro-Hungarian proposal, but also the Kosovo region, Ulqini, Plava and Guzije in Montenegro, and the Chameria region, including the coastal North part of Epirus, down to Preveza.

The Great Powers never losing sight of their own imperial interests, and in the absence of clear criteria, used the Albanian speaking territories to satisfy the demands of Albania's neighbours. None of these proposals submitted to the London Conference was fully implemented, and the Great Powers "compromised" in satisfying neither of the contending parties. Hence, half of Epirus – the Chameria region was given to Greece, but not its Northern part that remained in Albania. Kosovo with a population that was 90 percent Albanian was attached to Serbia; Plava, Guzia and Ulqini were handed to Montenegro, and the Eastern part of Lake Ohrid (today's Western part of North Macedonia) was attached to the new Serbian territory, which in the aftermath of the "Great War" became part of the Kingdom of Yugoslavia. Thus, the Conference was responsible for redrawing the Balkan map, a map which for Albanians failed to achieve its desire for full nation statehood and territorial integrity.

2.1: Proposed boundaries at the London Conference 1913

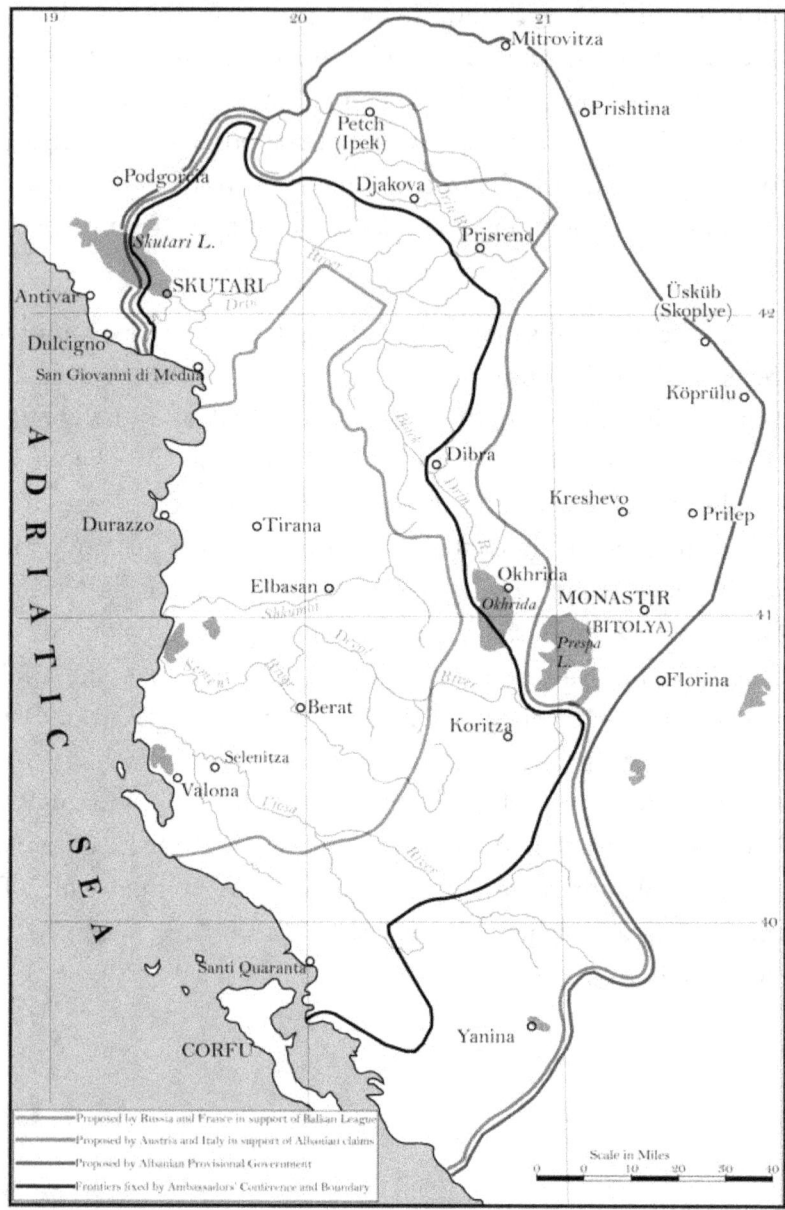

Source: Adopted proposed boundaries at the London Conference. Balkan Map 13, US Commission, DOS, RD 256; A similar version can also be found at H. C. Woods (1918), "Albania and Albanians", The Geographic Review, 5: 259, in Guy 2008:403.

Prelude to the Great War – Italy's struggle to assert its territorial ambitions

At the outbreak of the Great War, Italy landed a naval battery at Sazan island in October 1914 some seven months before Italy officially entered the war. In a secret agreement signed in London in April 1915, Italy pressured the Allies to recognize her occupation and thus sovereignty over Valona and Sazan which ironically remained under Italian control until August 1920 when as a result of anti-Italian sentiments breaking out in the neighbourhoods of Valona, Italy withdrew.

While Italy was close to the Balkans and Albania, it constantly struggled to assert its authority. In large part at the time, Italy lacked the force, resources and power to make its presence felt. In this period Albania acquired greater interest in the eyes of Italian leaders in terms of its colonial and imperial ambitions. Nonetheless Italy put on the table the desire to have the ports of Durazzo and Valona as compensation. The second Balkan war of 1913 brought again to the surface the Austro-Serb crisis this time over the Albanian border and on this occasion, Italy supported Austria on Albanian affairs as Italy and Austria could not afford to act separately. By 1914, Italy was ready to cooperate with Austria to forbid Serbian access to the Adriatic but equally to ensure that Austria would not be installed there either. Nonetheless Austria in 1914 and in secret, began putting an end to the Slav desires to find ways of reaching and accessing the Adriatic. These moves afoot were undertaken against Italian desires and as such put Italy against the Central powers – an event of profound importance given the divisions of the Great War that would immediately follow. Commenting on Italy's heightened period of colonial activities a decade after World War One, when related to Albania, Wickham Steed, journalist and editor of The Times offered the observation that:

> ...between 1897 and the summer of 1914, Italian policy in regard to Albania and the Balkans was a known quantity. Its

object was to prevent any change detrimental to Italian security; or, in the event of change, to secure for Italy advantages commensurate with any which Austria-Hungary might obtain (Wickham-Steed 1927).

As would emerge in 1915, as the Great War continued, Italy was still seeking redress to the Albania situation and at the secret Convention of London in April, Italy's demands on Albania were conceded. These included Italy having Sazan and Valona, the coast between this area under Italian sovereignty and Cape Stylos was to be neutralized. At the same time Serbia, Montenegro and Greece were to take up various parts of Albania and what was left would be a small autonomous Muslim state with Durazzo as its port and Italy to provide the "state keeping". The durability and reality of this outcome would need to wait for the end of the Great War in 1918. This would not turn out as many had desired.

Photo 1: Skanderbeg between 1600 and 1602 by Dominicus Custos
License: Public domain, Wikipedia Commons.

Photo 2:
Albanian Revolt 1910-La Tribuna Illustrata article from August 16, 1910
Licence: Public domain, Wikipedia Commons.

Photo 3:
Piana degli Albanesi (Palermo, Italy) 10 September 1911 - "Pro Albania" demonstration (In the center, the Poet Giuseppe Schirò; behind him Papàs Gaetano Petrotta).
Licence: Public domain, Wikipedia Commons.

Photo 4: Celebration of the first anniversary of the Albanian Declaration of Independence held on 28 November 1913.
Licence: Public domain, Wikipedia Commons.

Photo 5: The Italian Army in Albania, 1916-1918. An Italian 6inch gun battery along the Adriatic coast.
Licence: Public domain, Wikipedia Commons.

Albania and the Italian "partner"

Photo 6: The Ypi Government, 1921. The Albanian Government headed by Xhafer Ypi formed on 24 December 1921. From the left: Mehmed Konica, Spiro Koleka, Fan Noli, Ismail Haki Tatzati, Xhafer Ypi, Ahmet Zogu, Hysen Vrioni, Kolë Thaçi.
Licence: Public domain, Wikipedia Commons.

3

Albania and Italy: From the Great War to the end of World War Two

World War One – its consequences for Italy and the Balkans

Before Italy entered the First World War as an ally of Triple Entente (the side of Britain, France and Russia), the country was locked in a political battle for and against entering. While there were forces pushing for entry such as Italian nationalists Benito Mussolini, Marinetti and Gabriele D'Annunzio all ardent supporters of Italy joining the war, the Socialist Party initially sought to delay this decision. In the streets Italy's left-wing unions actively sought to stop Italian involvement in the war, organising strikes throughout 1914 against the war. In the early stages of the war, the Socialist Party and the Catholic Church were both on the side of no entry into the war and despite this opposition those for the war won the day and Italy joined the war in May 1915 on the side of the Entente.

In 1915 the Kingdom of Italy signed the London Treaty and as a concession for its involvement in the Great War, Italy was promised the two localities, Sazan Island and the town of Vlorë which Italy occupied. Part of the extra concessions for joining the war would involve having the rest of Albania as an Italian Protectorate. Despite this Italian claim and occupation, Austria-Hungary moved quickly and occupied almost the entirety of Albania. In 1915 Italy declared war on Austria and Hungary, and only declared war against Germany one year later. The secret treaty concessions in the end were never implemented partially because of the deteriorated relations between Italy with France and Britain as well as the public disclosure of the treaty by the Bolsheviks after taking power in November 1917. Austro-Hungary also made this secret treaty public in Albania, attempting to mobilise the Albanian population of the North against Serbs who had moved quickly to occupy Albania's North. By July 1917, Greece, Italy, Austria, France, Serbia and Montenegrin troops were all present in different parts of the Albania and once again Albania struggled against foreign ambitions of its territory.

Upon entering the war, Italy spread its occupation to the region of southern Albania, beginning in the autumn of 1916 recruiting Albanian irregulars to serve alongside Italian forces. With the permission of the Allied command, Italy also occupied Northern Epirus in August 1916, forcing the Greek Army to withdraw. In June 1917, Italy proclaimed central and Southern Albania as a protectorate while Northern Albania was allocated to Serbia and Montenegro. In late 1918, French and Italian forces expelled the Austro-Hungarian Army from Albania and Italy re-occupied the Vlorë harbour briefly to later withdraw after the Albanian resistance in 1920, known as 'Vlorë war'. Despite this outcome for Italy, in 1921 a decision of the Paris Conference of Ambassadors provided Italy with protectorate status of Albania which would allow Italy to have an inside running on Albania, especially with growing signs of a possible emergence of the new state of Yugoslavia.

Mistrust between Italy and Austria ran deep especially given the Habsburg Empire's attempts to thwart Italian unification. In exchange for its efforts and as a form of payback, Italy was offered South Tyrol (formerly part of Austria) and Venezia Giulia. Italy's entry into the Great War, was undertaken in what one scholar called "a spirit of bargain rather than crusade". It was also entry under the false understanding that "the war would be both short and advantageous" (Paxton 1975:110).

Within Italian society the Great War was placing the population under economic and social pressure. As a testimony to the deep-seated feeling of anger against the war, 41 people were killed during the summer bread riot in Turin in 1917 and many began calling for a compromise peace. Italy's involvement in the Great War, despite its brevity, still resulted in some 750,000 dead and its population at the war's end felt little sense of victory. The territorial gains were modest compared to the lives lost and the hardship suffered. Moreover, economic inequities continued to flourish across the peninsular ultimately sharpening social conflict. Inflation quadrupled during the war and inflated promises to returned soldiers only inflaming the situation. Industrial strikes, agrarian land seizures and demonstrations brought Italy close to social revolution. Compounding the discontent amongst Italians and especially returning Italian soldiers came also the most humiliating defeat in the locality of Caporetto in 1917 (now Kobarid in Slovenia), and world attention turned to developments in Russia with the October 1917 revolution where the Bolsheviks seized power and soon after agreed to peace with Germany. In November 1918 the guns were silenced and the Great War with all its carnage came to an end. Very few could genuinely rejoice.

Albania—an independent and dysfunctional state plunged into war

The Great Powers realized the enormous political challenges for the newly recognized Albania, a quasi-state. While Pro-Ottoman elements were still active in and around Albania, and the appetite of its neighbours, Greece and Serbia to make land grabs showed no signs of relenting, Austro-Hungarians lobbied the German Prince Wilhelm of Wied (Wilhelm Friedrich Heinrich 1876–1945), to rule over the Principality of Albania which he accepted. From March until his exile in September 1914, Wied, was officially recognised as King of Albania.

Upon acceptance of the throne in 1914, Wied travelled to the provisional capital, Durrës, and began the task of organising an Albanian government. He appointed Turhan Pasha Përmeti as the head of government which was mostly composed of aristocrats and Albanian notables such as Esat Pasha Toptani and other chieftains. Alongside a disastrous economic situation, the government was under pressure to protect Albania from both Serbia and Greece. From the Southeast, the Greek Army penetrated Albanian lands, encouraging a separatist movement of North Epirus, whereas, from the North, both the Montenegrin and Serbian Army continued to attack. In December 1913, the Council of Florence reminded all parties of the London Conference's findings on Albanian borders. By February 1914, the Greek government decided to comply with decisions made by the Council of Florence to halt their military attacks on Albania. Despite this, fighting continued between Albanian irregulars and Greece during the spring of 1914. The same happened to the North Albania where in the absence of a strong Albanian army, Albanians fought in irregular forces.

Wied's authority never extended much beyond Durrës, and his ability to protect South and North Albania was very limited. Italy considered Weid loyal to the Austro-Hungarians, and thus, a hurdle to its territorial ambitions in Albania. As a result, Italy financed Esat Pasha's plot to overthrow Wied in May 1914. The Italian plot was exposed and Esat Pasha was arrested, though later released and forced to go into exile. With the outbreak of the First World War, Austro-Hungary requested Wied to send Albanian troops to fight the Serbs alongside their allies. Wied's refusal marked the end of his support from the Austro-Hungarians, which also ended his reign of Albania. On 3 September 1914, Wied fled Albania to never return. Esat Pasha, a very controversial figure in the Albanian history, continued to be instrumental in Albanian politics of the time, and never stopped dreaming about the Albanian throne until his assassination by an Albanian student, Avni Rustemi in Paris in June 1920.

Italy rewarded for its war commitment

Being on the victorious side of the Great War, Italy's expansionist appetite increased. After the London Agreement, Italy never stopped in its efforts to seek gains from the Ottoman territory, especially Albania. Italy understood that its expansionist plans to occupy Albania without an agreement with Greece and especially Serbia would be futile. As a result, another post-war secret agreement between representatives of Greece, the Prime Minister Eleftherios Venizelos and the Italian Minister of Foreign Affairs, Tommaso Tittoni was signed (Bianchi 2018: 142). It stated that Greece promised to accept Italian claims over Vlorë and the Italian protectorate over Albania. On the other hand, Italy promised to support Greece's territorial claims over North Epirus, and Serbia to annex the Northern part of Albania (Stavrianos [1965] 2000: 710-2). Austro-Hungary and Italy were competing for more influence in the Northwest and the Adriatic. Yet again Albania found itself pulled apart by the competing powers.

In 1919, Edith Durham mentions that the strongest support for Albania, Austria, was close to joining Russia in opposing an Albanian nation-state and thus realise its interests in the Balkans (Durham 1919: 41). The Treaty of Versailles officially ended World War One in June 1919 and a few months later, the Paris Peace Treaty held by victorious allies decided on the peace terms for the defeated central powers. The Paris Treaty ignored the objection of the Albanian Provisional Government that Albanian speaking territories had been left out of the Albanian boundaries a feature repeated in both the Berlin Congress in 1878 and London Conference in 1913. Securing the borders of the weak Albanian State was and continued to be an ongoing challenge.

Italian fascism comes to power – The quest for Albania becomes more immediate

The beginning of 1918 saw another actor – the US, further its interest in European and world affairs through its President Woodrow Wilson, who in January 1918 addressed the US Congress on the new international order created by the end of World War One. In his speech Wilson, as it turned out, presented fourteen points, which were crucial for the survival and existence of the Albanian nation. These points emphasised self-determination, free trade and democracy in the new post-war world order. Point eleven of this presentation addressed the occupied territories in the Balkans that should be restored to the embryonic new nations and point twelve discussed the necessity to secure sovereignty of states that emerged from the Ottoman Empire. Wilson's speech and his fourteen points were instrumental in what would become the outcomes of the Treaty of Versailles between allies and Germany in 1919.

The Peace Conference of 1919 provided Italy with territorial claims which included Trentino, Istria and Trieste. To its annoyance, Italy's request for Dalmatia went to Yugoslavia while the city of Fiume was placed under international control. This unfavourable outcome for Italy unleashed nationalist expression including the seizure of the Port of Fiume by a group of soldiers led by nationalist leader and poet Gabriele D'Annunzio in September 1919, occupying the port until January 1921. The Italian government in conjunction with Yugoslavia were obliged to blockade the port forcing D'Annunzio and his followers to surrender.

In the early 1920s with the emergence of the new Soviet Union, some of the European powers along with the US and Japan provided assistance to the Russian White Army and the anti-Bolsheviks to stop the Bolshevik consolidation. On this they failed. Italy remained somewhat on the sidelines of these developments as it contended with its own domestic concerns and working-class trouble that was brewing at home.

After the war, many of the internal contradictions rose to the surface in Italy. Massive strike movements emerged between 1919 and 1920 – often called the "two red years" – which saw millions on strike. Confrontation with the police was a daily routine and between April 1919 and September 1920 some 320 protesters were killed. Strikes were also initiated against the Italian government's decision to recognise the leadership of the White Russian Kolchak and the activities of Western intervention against Soviet Russia. Factory councils sprang up with hundreds of thousands of workers involved in Milan and Turin which ultimately witnessed the prominence of Antonio Gramsci in what would become the precursor to the establishment of the Communist Party of Italy in 1921. What this revolutionary surge also did was brought fear and panic to the political elite, industrialists and the Italian middle and upper class that there needed to be a response to this threat. Emerging in the background was a growing nationalistic and anti-Bolshevik movement headed by Benito Mussolini which would come to the call and which in a matter of a few years would claim power in Italy. Fascism was on the cusp of taking power.

Mussolini comes to power

The rise of Benito Mussolini and his growing nationalist movement was in part a response to Italy's poor standing in the international grab for power. As soldiers returned home in 1918, Mussolini spoke bitterly about those veterans and what they found home after the war. Many witnessed the social crisis which had engulfed Italy and the stronger standing of the left-wing parties and unions. Mussolini, himself a former syndicalist inside the Socialist Party and editor of its paper Avanti in 1912, was eventually expelled from the party in 1914 when he called for Italy's entry into the war – a position the Socialist Party had been firmly opposed to. In 1919 Mussolini established his new political party in Milan, advancing a fascist program which drew attention to the left wing and unions as well as the threat of

Communism from the victory of the Bolsheviks in Russia. The ideas emerging were laced in nationalist rhetoric, territorial claims, institutional reform and removal, redistribution of land for the peasants and for the confiscation of Church property. Threatened by this social unrest, Mussolini encouraged his forces to act against the perpetrators of this social unrest. During 1920 and 1921 they took aim at the Socialist party, unions, farm labourers and cooperatives destroying their offices, and their press. The fascist ranks grew from 30,000 in 1920 to 300,000 by the end of 1922.

After the so-called "March on Rome" in October 1922, Victor Emmanuel III asked Mussolini to form a government. By the time of his coronation, Mussolini had formed a ministry ensuring he held the key posts of Foreign Affairs, the Interior and Justice ministry. At the same time, he made clear that the road had been cleared for the repression of Socialists and leftists of all stripes. Mussolini would declare this when in January 1925 he stated: "We wish to make the nation fascist" (Paxton 1975: 200). Industrialists, landowners, army officers and police were now able to make common cause to rid oppositionists and socialists and Mussolini's fascism began slowly gaining full control.

Mussolini's approach throughout the 1920s however failed to stabilise the economy as it kept deteriorating with the final blow being the world depression. By 1932 Italian unemployment had reached 20 percent and industrial production declined between 5-9 per cent. In the early 1930s, the crisis hit Italy's three key banks – Banca Commerciale, Credito Italiano and Banco di Roma. In response to this serious financial crisis, the Italian government assumed control of the banks and placed them under the umbrella of the *Istituto per la Ricostruzione Industriale* (IRI). While initiated as a temporary measure it eventually remained a government concern until its dissolution in 2022. This was one of the corporatist features of new fascist state.

Overall, the fascist period was characterized economically by a decline in trade throughout the late 1920s and into the 1930s as protectionist walls emerged and the country was again stalked by inflation and high levels of government deficits. From 1933 onwards, Italy moved towards an industrial society with industrial production now exceeding that of agriculture.

By 1926 with the assassination of Giacomo Matteotti, all parties except the Fascists had been dissolved, the death penalty had been restored and controls imposed on the press and freedom of association. It was now a consolidated fascist state and as the regime progressed into the next decade, the Monarchy, the Church and the Defence forces accepted the primacy of fascism. Further signs of this association were evidenced only a couple of years later with the Lateran Pact of 1929. This was an important achievement given the Church's break with Italy since the 1860s. The new agreement accorded the Catholic Church new authority and status and most importantly Italy's sole State religion.

Albanian survival through the inter-war years - dysfunctional state to monarchy

By the end of World War One, Albania was again partitioned and occupied by Serbian, Greek, French, British and Italian armies. Albanian leaders had neither the support nor the strength to oppose these armies. The dysfunctional government of Durrës was operating under Italian protection and could not extend its authority over the Northern tribal chieftains and Southern landowners. Nevertheless, Albanians sensed the danger of partition once more and tried to react. In their very last attempt, Albanian representatives from across Albania convened at the Congress of Lushnje from 21 January until 9 February 1920. The Congress of Lushnje aimed to protect Albanian lands against possible invasion from foreign armies. Although it did not have any authority, the Congress of

Lushnje operated on the besa approach, which according to the Albanian Kanun was the most powerful judicial institution for Albania. The Congress of Lushnje produced the first constitutional document and elected a four-man supreme council composed of a Catholic, an Orthodox a Sunny Muslim and a Bektashi. The Congress sent a letter to the Conference of Paris asking that Albanian territorial unity be protected, and decisions made by the London Conference in 1913 to draw up boundaries of Albania be reversed. The Congress also decided unanimously not to recognise the Durrës government, which was supported by Italy, and to lead the armed resistance against Italian and other occupations. These warnings of foreign involvement were vindicated when Italy again attacked the gulf of Vlorë in 1920, which resulted in an embarrassing defeat for Italian forces. Albanian morale received a boost when in December 1920 Albania was admitted into the League of Nations. Despite all these gestures one year later, under the authority of the Conference of Ambassadors (in effect the Great Powers) Italy was accorded the right to act in Albania.

Between 1920 and 1939 the Albanian state began to consolidate as an independent actor domestically and internationally. It was also a period characterised by a political rivalry between Fan Stilian Noli and Ahmet Zog. Noli was a Harvard-educated scholar who believed in parliamentary democracy while Ahmet Zog was an authoritarian figure educated at Lycée de Galatasaray in Constantinople (Istanbul) and leader of the important Mati tribe. Noli and Zog represented two different approaches - with Noli embracing Western ideology based on liberal democracy and Zog mirroring the authoritarian rule of Constantinople. Zog initially got the upper hand and took power in 1922, establishing an authoritarian regime that filled the political vacuum left in Albania after World War One. Although he was supported by some tribal leaders, his popularity was never significant, and, after the assassination of Avni Rustemi in April 1924, he began to lose legitimacy. The unrest of the so-called "June revolution" forced Zog to flee to Yugoslavia. As a result of this "revolution", the same month, a short-lived government led by the reformist Noli was appointed, but again overthrown by Zog six months later in December 1924 fleeing initially to Italy and then to the US. Zog assumed power with the backing of Albanian tribal supporters and the Yugoslav military. He valued the assistance from his Yugoslav supporters, and as a gesture of recognition, in June 1925, he ceded a small part of Albanian territory called "Saint Naum Monastery" to Yugoslavia (Pearson 2005: 248). In addition, Zog loyalties to higher masters was demonstrated by his allowing, as per a secret agreement between Serbia and Turkey, to de-populate Kosovo. This project was initiated in 1937 by a Serbian academic, Vasa Cubrillovic [Čubrilović], known as "Iseljavanje Arnauta" [The expulsion of the Albanians] (Cohen 2013: 44), which, according to Kadare, "shows its explicit aim in its very title" (Kadare 2011: 33). As a result, in 1938, Turkey accepted that 40,000 Albanian families be transferred from Kosovo to Turkey.

Despite his contribution to consolidate an Albanian state, Zog was a monarch and declared himself the King of Albania in 1928. He remained attached to his "declared" throne until 7 April 1939 when Italy occupied Albania forcing Zog to flee. It was not a surprise for Victor Emmanuel III to receive the crown of Albania alongside that of Ethiopia from the colonial expansion wars conducted by Mussolini.

Italy's thirst for colonial conquests and *"La Quarta sponda"*

During the 1930s the Italian fascist government expanded its colonial ambitions with the conquering of Abyssinia in 1936 which produced ineffective sanctions from the League of Nations. On the eve of the Second World War, Italy expanded its war machine and raised its military expenditure to 9.5 per cent of total government expenditure. Despite this investment, in 1939 the Italian economy was in no position to sustain a war, but fascist military ambitions ignored these warnings. Military preparations were now in progress.

3.1: *Navigazione Adriatica* – Albanian Lines 1937

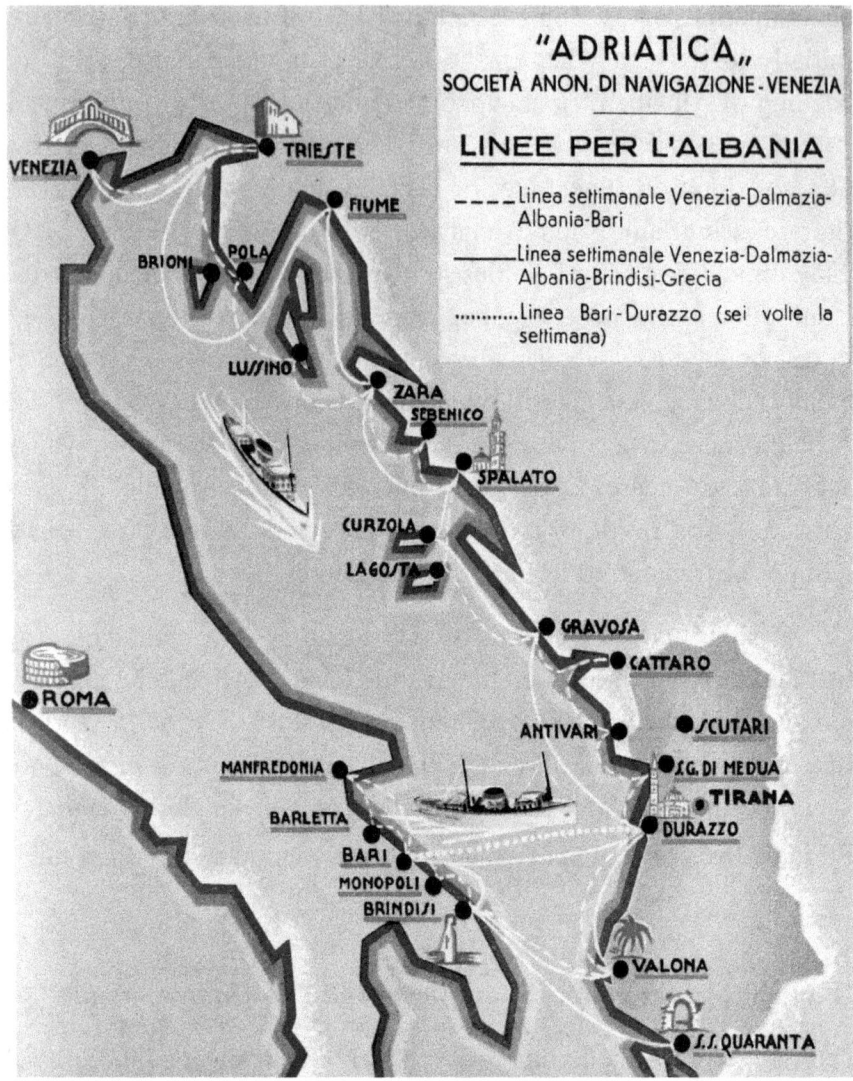

Map of the ferry lines operated by the state-owned Italian steamship company *"Societa per Azioni di Navigazione Adriatica,"* usually referred to as Adriatica, 1937. License: Public domain, Wikipedia Commons

In the lead up to Italy's invasion of Albania in 1939, the Italian Fascist regime had politically and economically penetrated and dominated Albania during Zog's rule and was planning for annexation of Albania years prior to the event. Albania became a de facto protectorate of Italy after the signing of the Treaties of Tirana of 1926 and 1927. Under Zog, Albania's economy was dependent on multiple financial loans given from Italy since 1931.

In August 1933, Mussolini placed stringent demands on Zog in exchange for Italy's continued support of Albania, including that all new appointments to leading positions in the Albanian government receive an "Italian education"; that an Italian expert be in all Albanian government ministries and that Italy take control of Albania's military. Italy also requested that any British officers training Albania's military be replaced by Italian officers; and that Albania must annul all of its existing commercial treaties with other countries and make no new agreements without the approval of the Italian government; and that Albania sign a commercial convention that would make Italy Albania's "most favoured country" in trade. In 1934 when Albania failed to deliver a scheduled payment of an Italian loan, Italian warships were sent off the coast of Albania as a form of intimidation.

On 25 August 1937, Italian foreign minister Count Ciano wrote in his diary of Italy's relations with Albania and the Duce's desire to move on Albania stating: "As we have avenged Adowa, so we will avenge Valona. Albania will become Italian. I cannot yet – and I do not wish to – tell you how or when. But it will happen" (Ciano Diary 1952: 201). One year later in 1938, Ciano spoke of annexing Albania like Germany had done with Austria:

> A report from Jacomoni on the situation in Albania. Our penetration is becoming steadily more intense and more organic. The programme which I traced after my visit is being carried out without a hitch. I am wondering whether the general situation – particularly the Anschluss [with Austria] – does not permit us to take a step forward towards the more complete domination of this country, which will be ours (Ciano Diary 1952: 94).

3.2: Albania in 1939-1944

License: Creative Commons Attribution-Share Alike 3.0, Wikipedia Commons.

The Italian fascist government invades Albania in 1939

Faced with Franco's imminent victory in Spain and Germany's quick intended moves in Europe, Mussolini did not wish to be looking flat-footed and therefore total control of Albania was now on the agenda. In spite of Albania's long-standing protection and alliance, and with the Albania economy totally controlled by Italy, on 7 April 1939 (Good Friday) Italian troops invaded Albania, five months before the start of the Second World War. The Albanian armed resistance proved ineffective against the Italians and, the country was quickly occupied forcing Albanian King Zog I to flee to Greece two days later. Following the King's departure, the Albanian Parliament, and under Italian pressure, forced the dethronement of Zog I and passed the crown rule to the King of Italy, Victor Emmanuel III who would remain King until Italy's surrender to the Allies in 1943. Throughout the Italian occupation political forces as well as pro-Communist elements fought to interrupt Italian occupation plans. Although Albania had been a de facto Italian protectorate since 1927, Mussolini wanted more direct control over the country. Mussolini's intention was to increase his and Italy's prestige, provide a response to Germany's annexation of Austria and its occupation of Czechoslovakia, and to have firm control over Albania to station large forces of the Italian military for future operations involving Yugoslavia and Greece. As a military conquest the occupation was insignificant, but it provided Italy with total control of the Adriatic leading closer to Italy's desire of making the Mediterranean "an Italian Lake" (Rowland 1972). The Corporative Council of the Albanian Fascist Party, a quasi-state organization, issued a directive on 16 June 1940, shortly after Italy's declaration of war against Britain and France, that stated that "The Kingdom of Albania considers itself at war with all nations against which Italy is at war—at present or in the future".

As an Italian protectorate, Albania was subordinated to Italian interests, the Albanian crown was declared in personal union with the Italian crown, Albania was to be governed by an Italian vice-regent representing King Victor Emmanuel III, a customs union was enacted, and Albanian foreign policy was to be handled by Rome. The Albanian armed forces were subsumed in the Italian military, Italian advisors were placed within all levels of the Albanian administration, and the country fascisticized with the establishment of an Albanian Fascist Party modelled after the Italian prototype. Italian citizens began to settle in Albania as colonists and to own land so that they could gradually transform it into Italian soil.

While Victor Emmanuel ruled as king, Shefqet Vërlaci served as the Prime Minister. Vërlaci controlling the day-to-day activities of the Italian protectorate. On 3 December 1941, Vërlaci was replaced as Prime Minister and Head of Government by Mustafa Merlika-Kruja. The country's natural resources too came under direct control of Italy with all petroleum resources absorbed by Italy's state petroleum company, AGIP. In 1939, Count Ciano spoke of Albanian irredentist claims to Kosovo as valuable to Italy's objectives, saying:

> The Kosovars [are] 850,000 Albanians, strong of body, firm in spirit, and enthusiastic about the idea of a Union with their Homeland. Apparently, the Serbians are terrified of them. ... But later one must adopt a politics of deep interest in Kosovo. This will help to keep alive in the Balkans an irredentist problem which will polarize the attention of the Albanians themselves and be a knife at the back of Yugoslavia (Ciano, 1939 cited in Zollo 2002).

Albania was important culturally and historically to the nationalist aims of the Italian Fascists, as the territory of Albania had long been part of the Roman Empire. The Italian Fascist regime legitimized its claim to Albania through studies proclaiming the racial affinity of Albanians and Italians, especially as opposed to the Slavic Yugoslavs. Italian Fascists claimed that Albanians were linked through ethnic heritage to Italians due to links with the prehistoric Italiotes, Illyrian and Roman populations. Albania's less than twenty years of independence could not prepare it for the storms that were on the horizon with Fascist Italy's invasion and occupation in 1939. Along with other designs from the Axis alliance, Albania would be subjected to a loss of national awareness and control and at the same time open up its resistance to axis military exploits which would change the course of Albanian independence and statehood which it would exploit in 1944.

Mussolini declares war against the Allies and attacks Greece

The Italian invasion of Albania in 1939 was already a warning sign for the Balkan nations and aroused suspicion especially from Serbia and Greece as to the Italian intentions. It also hit a note of concern from France and Britain about Italy's undeclared ambitions. The Greek Prime Minister at the time, Ioannis Metaxas, was ideologically sympathetic to Mussolini. Despite reassurances from Italian diplomatic sources, "The Greeks… were not reassured; they feared that the seizure of Albania might be a prelude to an attack on Greece…" (Cervi, 1971: 3). Strategically, control of Albania gave Italy an important beachhead in the Balkans: not only did it complete Italian control of the Strait of Otranto and the entrance to the Adriatic Sea, but it could also be used to invade either Yugoslavia (in tandem with another thrust via Venezia Giulia) or Greece.

In June 1940, Mussolini declared war on his ex-allies France and Great Britain. He then sent an ultimatum to Greece in October of the same year requesting Greece hand over parts of its territory. Mussolini planned to invade Greece and other countries like Yugoslavia in the area to give Italy territorial control of most of the Mediterranean Sea coastline, as part of the Fascists' objective of creating the objective of Mare Nostrum ("Our Sea") in which Italy would dominate the Mediterranean. Metaxas rejected the Italian request and once the ultimatum expired, Italian troops based in Albania, occupied Northern Greece. Although Italian troops penetrated Greek territory, they were halted by the resistance of the Greek Army on the Albanian-Greek border and, soon after the Italian invasion, Greece counter-attacked and a sizable portion of Albania entered Greek hands (including the cities of Gjirokastër and Korçë). In little more than a month, Greek resistance managed to stop Italian advances inside Greek territory.

By the end of winter and the beginning of spring in 1941, the Greek Army was able to push the Italian forces back, forcing the Italians to reorganise their forces for another attack from Albania. The Albanian army under the command of colonel (later general) Prenk Pervizi abandoned the Italians in combat, causing a major unravelling of their lines. The Albanian army believed to be the cause of the betrayal was removed from the front. Colonel Pervizi and his staff of officials were isolated in the mountains of Pukë and Shkodër to the North. This was the first effective action of revolt against the Italian occupation. In April 1941, Greece capitulated after an overwhelming German invasion. As such all of Albania returned to Italian control, alongside most of Greece, now jointly occupied by Italy, Germany and Bulgaria. Greek troops were now attacking Albania from Korcë to Gjirokastër, arriving close to Vlorë. Britain was quick to send aid to the Greek Army, but this could not support large numbers of Greek soldiers and reserve forces for the entire summer. Hitler, aware of the danger posed by Britain in Greece, invaded Northern Greece in April 1941. Greek troops then surrendered to the Germans on 20 April.

German occupation of Albania at first tried to avoid full scale confrontation with the Albanian resistance. After the collapse of fascist Italy in July 1943, with only two divisions and minimum effort, Nazi-Germany occupied Albania until winter 1944. After "neutralizing" part of the Albanian resistance movement, in November 1943 the German military decided to move on the active brigades of Albanian resistance. In late 1944 the USSR began taking the offensive in the Balkans forcing German units to leave Greece and Albania and by the end of November 1944 there were no more German units left inside Albanian territory.

The rise of the Albanian Communist Party and Enver Hoxha

The effects of the October Revolution in 1917 and the rise of communist ideas, spread to Europe, the Balkans and Albania soon after. The first Albanian communist cell created in Korçë in 1927, was soon followed by other cellules of Shkodër and Tirana. The future Albanian communist leader, Enver Hoxha, studied at the French High School of Korçë (Le Lycée de Korça) from 1927 until 1930. He secured a scholarship in 1934 from the Albanian government to study in France but lost the scholarship due to his poor academic performance. After two years of roaming Europe, he returned to Albania in 1936. During his time in France, he embraced communist ideas. In France, he met one of his later opponents, Isuf Luzaj who was a student at the University of Sorbonne from 1931. In 1936, Luzaj graduated from the University of Sorbonne with two PhD's, one in literature and the other one in Philosophy and returned to Albania. Upon his return to Albania, he was employed as a teacher at the Teaching Institute of Elbasan and then the French High School of Korcë.

In 1938 Luzaj was arrested then released for publishing his first book, Rrefimet, where in his poem "Neroni" he criticised Zog's regime for its spread of hunger in Albania. Luzaj, who had embraced liberal ideas in France was a social justice activist. After Korçë's hunger march in 1938, he was then transferred to Vlorë as punishment for spreading communist ideas amongst protesters. Luzaj was a patriot, strong supporter of the hunger strike and liberal ideas. With the Italian invasion in April 1939, Luzaj was amongst those who resisted the occupation but was soon arrested and sent to jail in Gjirokastër until March 1940, and then sent to the Italian prison camp of Ventotene, from where he was released in August 1942. While in jail, Luzaj met some Albanian nationalist elements who were not in support of the communist programme and formed their own political grouping, *Balli Kombëtar*. Luzaj then returned to Vlorë in Autumn 1942, but soon was forced to hide in the mountains after fascists discovered his intention to mobilise his ex-students against the fascist regime. From the *labëria* mountains of South Albania, he then led the armed resistance of the *Balli Kombëtar*.

Hoxha on the other hand was also employed at the French School from where he started to openly express communist ideas and later became an active member of the Communist Group of Korcë, supporting also Albanian uprisings against the Zog monarchy. In a short period of time communist groups started to collaborate and share information with other communist forces across Albania. Although the communist movement in Albania suffered a setback in 1939, after Zog's troops arrested and imprisoned most of the members of the Shkodër Group, help from communists from neighbouring countries provided relief including being active in Albania.

In the meantime, the French School of Korçë attracted attention from the Italian regime and Mussolini had it closed down in 1939 with the future leader Enver Hoxha losing his job. In order to protect him, the Communist Group of Korçë sent him to support revolutionary activities alongside the Tirana Group. The task of unification against Italian fascists became imminent. Therefore, despite factions and divisions, communist Albanians managed to form the Albanian Communist Party, *Partia Komuniste Shqiptare* (PKSH), in 1941. It is known this was done with the participation and support of two Yugoslav Communist Party delegates, Dushan Mugosha and Miladin Popovic (Skendi 1957: 77).

Another prominent Albanian who played an important role in this period was Musine Kokalari – a close-relative of Hoxha and known as the first Albanian female writer to have published in the linguistic field. Kokalari graduated in modern literature from La Sapienza University (Rome) in 1942. She embraced anti-fascist ideas in Italy, and upon her return to Albania in 1942, Kokalari attempted to join the high ranks of the PKSH. Kokalari found incompatibility between PKSH and her own ideas. Kokalari, soon realised that her ideas about social justice were very close to those of Luzaj and Skënder Muco, deciding to form another political entity in Autumn 1943, the Albanian Social-Democratic Party. Her aim was to unite the Albanian Anti-Fascist and National Liberation Movement (*Lëvizja Antifashiste Nacional-Çlirimtare*) known as LANÇ with *Balli Kombëtar* in a united political organisation to fight invading troops. Kokalari's strong social justice beliefs were embedded in the Social-Democratic Party programme, which spoke about free speech and religious freedom to all Albanians.

The increasing activity of the Albanian resistance movement did not go unnoticed by British intelligence services in the Balkans. British pressure produced a meeting of various Albanian resistance groups in August 1943 where PKSH and *Balli Kombëtar* tried to resolve their differences in the Conference of Mukje. While both, the PKSH and *Balli Kombëtar* fought for Albanian liberation of Albania from all foreign powers, *Balli Kombëtar* also proposed the national unification of all Albanians, a request initially accepted by the PKSH. Yugoslavia aimed at keeping Kosovo within their federation, and the request of "national unity" from *Balli Kombëtar* did not suit them.

The agreement declared its intention to pursue full independence which would include an "ethnic Albania" together with Kosovo. Under the pressure from the Communist Party of Yugoslavia, Hoxha rejected the Mukje proceedings on national unification, joining several days later the meeting of the Central Committee of the Communist Party of Albania in Labinot. After this episode, due to strong support from the Yugoslav communists, the PKSH became the leadership of the LANÇ. After the Mukje conference, members of *Balli Kombëtar* were not welcomed in talks with the PKSH anymore, as they were identified as anti-communists. Abaz Kupi, a member of the LANÇ who participated in the conference and felt that only the return of Zog would result in national unity, was expelled by LANÇ to then create the Legality Movement.

By November 1943, Hoxha became the leader of LANÇ and declared war on *Balli Kombëtar*, as well as on the Legality Movement led by a Royal officer—Abaz Kupi loyal to Zog. The LANÇ was now fighting the Germans, *Balli Kombëtar* and the *Legaliteti* (Legality) resistance—a situation that suited Germany which supported forces opposed to the communists. In December 1943, the Albanian government used its army to support the Germans – a move welcomed by the Reich. From November 1943 until June 1944, the German-supported Albanian government was led by a nationalist leader of *Balli Kombëtar*, Rexhep Mitrovica. After his resignation, the Germans appointed another Prime Minister from *Balli Kombëtar* who had links with *Legaliteti*, Fiqiri Dine, who also resigned on 29 August 1944 to allow another pro-German, and the third member of *Balli Kombëtar*, Ibrahim Bicaku, to become the Albanian Prime Minister under German occupation. The differences in ideology between LANÇ on one hand, and *Balli Kombëtar* and *Legaliteti* on the other, was now becoming clearer.

It was then easy for Hoxha to become the Head of the Albanian provisional government at the Congress of Përmet in May 1944. The PKSH took an active role in the Albanian resistance that lasted until winter 1944 when German troops left Albania. This was followed by allied bombardments and partisan attacks from Greece, Albania and Yugoslavia. It was expected that the PKSH would take matters into their own hands given that *Balli Kombëtar* and *Legaliteti* were no longer able to count on the support from the German occupation which was no more.

By November 1944, the Albanian Communist Party, which had led the Albanian resistance against Italian and German occupation, became the leading force in the country. Most leaders of *Balli Kombëtar* and Legality, including Abaz Kupi and Luzaj realised the danger of the communists coming to power and fled Albania. The PKSH began a systematic campaign of prosecuting their opponents and some like Kokalari understood the danger that would come her way given both her brothers were killed without trial and others from her family disappeared. Kokalari, or what Luzaj calls in one of his poems "the icon of the Albanian history" (Luzaj ND 2020) was imprisoned for 30 years by the Hoxha regime and died in misery in 1983. The other Albanian prominent philosopher and writer, Luzaj fled to Italy, to then migrate to Argentina and later to the US from where he published around 150 books and essays in philosophy and linguistics. He left his wife and five children in Albania, and only reunited with them in 1990. Literature on both Kokalari and Luzaj is not widely known in Albania. Nevertheless, they were both two great Albanian scholars who were purged by their main opponent, Enver Hoxha.

The Italian collapse and Albania during World War II

After the fall of Yugoslavia and Greece in April 1941, the Italian government began negotiations with Germany, Bulgaria, and the newly established client state, the Independent State of Croatia, on defining their borders. In April Mussolini called for the borders of Albania to be expanded – including annexing Montenegro into Albania that would have an autonomous government within Albania, and expanding Albania's border eastwards, though not as far as the Vardar River as some had proposed – citing that Ohrid should be left to the Slavic Macedonians, regardless of whether Vardar Macedonia would become an independent state or be annexed by Bulgaria. However, the Italian government changed its mind on the border, later supporting the annexation of Ohrid and giving the territory directly outside of Ohrid (including the sacred birthplace of Saint Clement) to the Slavic Macedonians. After some negotiations, Italy's new Balkan borders – including Albania's new borders, were officiated by royal decree on 7 June 1941.

In July 1943, as the Allies were preparing their landing in Sicily, news arrived of the arrest of Mussolini and instalment of General

Badoglio as the new Italian commander of Italian forces. Eventually on 8 September 1943 Italy declared its surrender to the Allies and the declaration of war against Germany. On the Albanian front this surrender involved some 130,000 troops that were still stationed there. Like disbanded Italian soldiers elsewhere, they either deserted the army, were taken as prisoners of war by the Germans, or joined the new anti-German alliance. Fugitive soldiers were often protected by Albanian families and, on occasion, joined the Albanian partisans in the fight for national liberation. Albanian communist partisans, with Allied logistics and material support, liberated Albania in 1944. Once the Germans were made aware of Italy's intentions, like they did elsewhere, they moved their 21st German Army to occupy Italian territories including that of Albania. Troops from Montenegro and Greece quickly moved to Albania to take control of areas that had formerly been part of the Italian occupation. The collapse of Italy on Albanian soil provided the resistance groups opportunities to seize arms and weapons which had been abandoned. In 1944 Badoglio declared Italy would no longer interfere in Albanian affairs.

By late 1944 the future of Albania was being determined through standoff between large contingents of partisans. The position of the Communist units was full independence and alternative organisations including smaller elites loyal to the former Zog reign had to decide which way to go. Some joined the partisans; others left the country. By 1945 the new Albanian communist supported government under the leadership of Enver Hoxha was established and Yugoslavia immediately recognised it. Other recognition came from France and most importantly, Italy. Others in Europe were less convinced, and Greece showed open animosity given that Albania was still supporting the communists in the Greek civil war between 1944 and 1949.

The rise of Tito's Yugoslavia

Tito emerged from the Second World War immensely popular both within and without Yugoslavia. The victorious partisan movement, different from many countries in Eastern Europe which were occupied by the USSR, provided a genuine military response to the Axis occupying forces. Moreover, it's merger between national independence and a social movement, fighting against the Germans, the Italians but also against the ultra-nationalistic forces of Serbian Chetniks and the Croatian *Ustasha* provided some remedy to the inter-ethnic brutality. Tito, a Slovene-Croat managed for the first time in their history to bring together all members of the Yugoslav nation in the fight for a common cause. While the early partisan movement was primarily supported by Serbs and the uprising initially began in Serbia, Croats eventually joined in larger numbers after 1941. The only ethnic group which played a minor role in the partisan movement were the Albanians of Kosovo (Crnobrnja 1994).

In late 1943 the partisan forces under the umbrella of the Anti-Fascist Alliance of Yugoslavia convened to discuss the future state of Yugoslavia. It was to be a Federal State made up of six Republics. At the end of the war in November 1945 this proposal would be sanctioned by the first Parliament of the new state which would emerge and would be in alignment with ideological Communist principles. The first election in January 1946, which removed the Royal Family, and not surprisingly won by the Communist led National Front, was "manipulated by the CPY [Communist Party of Yugoslavia] ... unnecessarily so since the popularity of Tito and the partisans would have easily led them to a comfortable victory..." (Crnobrnja 1994: 68). Tito as premier from 1945, ensured that Serbian and Croatian nationalists would be less influential in the new Yugoslavia and by having Serb nationalist leader Mihajlovi executed and seeing *Ustasha* supporter Archbishop Stepinac of Zagreb jailed, would send a clear message of this intention.

4

The Cold War: Albania's different path from Yugoslavia and Italy

As the new Yugoslavia took shape in 1945, it was clear that internal ethnic matters required addressing especially with the larger Serbian presence in the Federation. Tito's intent was to scale Serbia's role downwards without infringing on their rights – an approach which was generally successful. At the same time, Yugoslavia began pursuing economic, internal, and foreign policy objectives which were in line with their Socialist approach but not necessarily in alignment with those of the USSR. One such matter was the admission of Albania into the Yugoslav Federation. Stalin was not keen on this conglomeration of Albania with Yugoslavia which ultimately failed but created even greater levels of insecurity within the Albanian political leadership. Another source of tension with the USSR was Yugoslavia's support for the Communists in the Greek Civil War which was not a policy supported by Stalin. The break between Yugoslavia and the USSR, which eventually came in 1948, had other ramifications including a significant disruption to the Yugoslav economy, which had depended on the USSR for economic support. Ultimately this change caused Yugoslavia to turn to the West for economic assistance and trade outlets.

As a result of the Stalin-Tito split between 1948 and 1951, many pro-Soviet elements within the Yugoslav Communist Party suffered. Curiously, the majority of the pro-Soviet elements purged from the party were mostly Serbs and Montenegrins and even more ironical, the Minister responsible for the purges was himself a Serb! Tito and the Yugoslav Communist Party began introducing new economic measures into Yugoslavia which had the effect of distancing itself from its original Socialist model. In the early 1950s Yugoslavia introduced a "self-management" economic model which lasted until 1965 moving away from a centrally planned approach to a local decisions structure. During this period economic growth grew and was higher than in most Eastern European countries but below that of Western Europe. This economic model later drew closer to what became known as "market socialism" which ultimately meant drawing closer to a fully-fledged capitalist system. The party, after the mid-1960s, began to see a greater role for business and less of the party, thereby marginalising the role of workers and managers in the workplaces. Throughout the Tito period, and given the intensity of the Cold War, Yugoslav foreign policy would be marked by an ideological closeness to the East while drawing economically closer to the capitalist West. One of Tito's main bearers was his support to the "Non-aligned" countries meaning neither with the USSR nor the USA.

Tito died in 1980 after 35 years at the helm. What can be said for the Tito years, especially after World War Two, was his hero status and undisputed leader with deep loyalty and admiration from the army and generally throughout Yugoslav society. Equally his ability to find ways and means to better integrate the six Republics and to do so without recourse to ethnic divisions. During the Tito years, there were few inter-ethnic disputes and as one observer noted "the national question did not raise its head" (Crnobrnja 1994: 76).

With the Albanian Communist Party taking state power, it quickly generated reactions by both Western and Eastern countries. The US, British and Allied governments requested that there be democratic elections, and alongside the Soviet Union, refused to recognise the communist Albanian Provisional Government until November 1945

(Pearson 2005: 477-8). Between 1944 and 1945, opposition political forces barely existed in Albania. Kokalari urged Allied forces to extend elections until the formation of a communist opposition was ignored by British representatives who felt that the communists deserved merit for fighting the Nazis. In one of his later interviews, Luzaj admitted that the communists were better placed to govern due to their better structure and the fact that some feudal *Balli Kombëtar* leaders from North Albania were not interested in fighting the German occupation and had collaborated with the Nazi-Germans (Luzaj ND 2020). As such there was little resistance to the Albanian Communist Party taking power officially after their electoral victory. Since the declaration of Independence in 1912, Albania had finally created the strongest state to oppose endless attempts by its neighbours to split the small and fragile Albania. However, Hoxha's rise to power also came with political costs which would emerge in the coming decades.

At the end of World War Two, Albania found itself at war with Greece, in effect a continuation of the Italian fascist invasion of Greece from Albanian territories in October 1940. Similar to Albania, Greece's main resistance in World War Two came from the communist guerrilla units of the National Liberation Front–National Popular Liberation Army (*Ethnikón Apeleftherotikón Métopon–Ethnikós Laïkós Apeleftherotikós Strátos)*, known as EAM-ELAS. The right wing, the Greek Democratic National Army (*Ellínikos Dímokratikos Ethnikós Strátos*) well known as EDES did only stop fighting the EAM-ELAS after the National Bands Agreement in May 1943, and under the British leadership an organised resistance against Germans had now commenced. As Germany withdrew from Greece, mass expulsion of more than 20,000 Muslim Albanians living in the Chameria region in 1944 followed. Worth noting was that after the German withdrawal, the majority of the massacres, and expulsions of Albanian-Muslim-Chams were conducted by the EDES right-wing forces led by Napoleon Zervas, who, with British support, secured all Ionian coast inhabited by Albanian Christian and

Muslim Chams. The expulsion of Albanian-Chams by Greece was not for the stated reason of their so-called collaboration with Germany, but rather to hide the existence of the Albanian minority in Greece—and the policy of protecting the rights of the Muslim Chams, Greece was in no position to implement despite its agreement with the Treaty of Lausanne in 1923 (Baltsiotis 2011: 19-20). A further demonstration of this abuse was demonstrated in 1946 where the US and UK governments noted Zervas' "wartime collaboration" and his "dictatorial ambitions" (Iatrides & Wringley 1995: 137). On the other hand, Albanian Christian Chams were simply registered as Greeks and thus, assimilated. The declaration of war with Albania by Greece in 1940 was still in force and thereby prohibiting Albanian Chams to return to their lands that were now part of Greece.

In 1946 the Greek Army was again penetrating the Albanian South-East thereby Tito, Albania's main supporter at the time, to consider sending two army divisions to shore Albanian defences. This fraternisation between Yugoslavia and Albania changed in December 1947 with the revelation of the Yugoslav plan for the annexation of Albania and for it to become the "Seventh Republic of Yugoslavia" (Pearson 2006: 242-3). The deputy Prime Minister and the Minister of Interior, Koçi Xoxe, who was supported by other pro-Yugoslav elements, agreed that the Albanian economy and military should unite with Yugoslavia. Moreover, the deterioration of relations between Belgrade and Moscow in June 1948, after the expulsion of Yugoslavia from the Communist Information Bureau (Cominform) also coincided with a marked change in relations between Albania and Yugoslavia. For his pro-Yugoslav sentiments, Xoxe was arrested and executed in 1949. The following decade saw significant attempts by the Albanian Communist Party to eradicate pro-Yugoslav elements.

Albania also found itself in contrast with the British government over the incident in the Channel of Corfu in October 1946 that resulted in damage to a British Navy vessel and the death of British military personnel. The US followed suit by suspending diplomatic relations with Albania in November 1946. As a consequence, Hoxha considered both Britain and the US as a threat to Albania, plunging tensions between them to greater depths after failed attempts by both the US and the UK to challenge Hoxha's regime between 1949 and 1952. During these years of tension with the US and the UK, the Soviet Union lent a hand of support though this too would not last.

The state of affairs at the end of the War

In the case of Italy, no diplomatic relations existed between them and many diplomatic disputes remained unresolved. Despite this tentative situation, and only days before Italian Liberation in April 1945, the Under Secretary of State of War, Mario Palermo visited Albania on behalf of the new Italian state. He reported on the state of Italian citizens left in Albania – a task he was permitted to do by the Albanian authorities. At the end of the war in 1945, there were some 27,000 Italians military and civilians still in Albania (Pandelejmoni 2017). Palermo's task was to assess the status of the Italian citizens including those organised through the *Circolo Garibaldi*, the Gramsci Brigade and other civilians spread across the country. Palermo indicated in his reports that with the exception of the Italian partisans, most Italians were in serious human difficulty. Moreover, he confirmed that Albania was to all intents and purposes a communist state (Pandelejmoni 2017).

Palermo secured an agreement with the Albanian leadership, including Hoxha, for a 12-point program mostly around the return of Italians back home. As a result of this agreement most Italians were repatriated to Italy. Those that remained were primarily specialists which Albania insisted were needed for national reconstruction. When the British Foreign Office was informed of the agreement, they were concerned that Italy had succumbed to an indirect recognition of the new communist state in Albania which other western allies were avoiding. Equally there was concern about the propaganda carried out by the Italian Communist Party amongst the Italian military in Albania and how this was undermining the pressure being placed on the new communist state in Albania. Little of this concerned Mario Palermo, who not surprisingly, was himself a member of the Communist Party. However, within a matter of a few years Italy too would adhere to the non-recognition of the Albania Communist State.

1947 Paris Peace treaty – Italy abandons claims to all its former colonies

One of the carryover tasks after the Second World War was addressing the punishment and injustices that had occurred during the war. This was undertaken through the 1947 Paris Peace Treaty. The treaty involved the wartime Allied powers negotiating the details of peace treaties with Italy, Romania, Hungary, Bulgaria and Finland. The negotiation and ultimately the settlement involved the responsibilities of the defeated that had inflicted damage and losses on other nations, including war reparation payments, respect for minority groups and territorial adjustments. The themes of redress also included the end of the Italian colonial empire in Africa, Greece, and Albania, as well as changes to the Italian–Yugoslav, Hungarian–Czechoslovak, Soviet–Romanian, Hungarian–Romanian, French–Italian, and Soviet–Finnish borders. The treaties also required handing over accused war criminals to the Allied powers. For Italy there were important settlements and agreements which required clarification. These included frontier changes as well as other internal political changes. Despite annoyance and disappointment, the Italian government reluctantly and with little choice, accepted the treaty recommendations. The outcome of the Conference from the Italian perspective was that Italy lost the colonies of Italian Libya and Italian East Africa. The latter consisted of Italian Ethiopia, Italian Eritrea, and Italian Somaliland. Italy continued to govern the former Italian Somaliland as a UN trust territory until 1960. In the Peace Treaty. This included the recognition of Albania as an "eternal" sovereign country, agreed to pay for war reparations to the tune of $US 5 million and to relinquish control over the island of Sazan (Czekalski 2013:30). Italy also lost its concession in Tianjin, which was turned over to China, and the Dodecanese Islands were ceded back to Greece. Italy lost Istria, and the provinces of Fiume, Zara, and most of Gorizia and Pola were ceded to Yugoslavia. The rest of Istria and the province of Trieste formed a new sovereign State (Free Territory of Trieste) divided in two administrative zones under a provisional government for which the United Nations Security Council was responsible. In 1954, Italy incorporated the Province of Trieste (Zone A) and Yugoslavia incorporated the rest of Istria (Zone B). This would be officially recognized through the Treaty of Osimo in 1975. The villages of the Tende valley and La Brigue were ceded to France, but Italian diplomats were able to maintain in place the Treaty of Turin (1860), according to which the French-Italian alpine border passes through the summit of Mont Blanc, despite French demands on the Aosta Valley. The province of South Tyrol was also kept by Italy despite the territorial demands of Austria, largely thanks to the Gruber–De Gasperi Agreement signed some months before.

Besides the territorial changes, Italy was obliged to pay war reparations to Yugoslavia, Greece, the Soviet Union, Ethiopia and Albania. The Treaty also demanded the removal of fortifications and banned Italy from possessing, building or experimenting with atomic weapons, guided missiles, guns with a range of over 30 km, non-contact naval mines and torpedoes as well as manned torpedoes. Equally the Italian military would be limited in size and would only be permitted to a maximum of 200 heavy and medium tanks. Former officers and non-commissioned officers of the Black shirts and the National

Republican Army were barred from becoming officers or non-commissioned officers in the Italian military (except those exonerated by the Italian courts). Equally, the Italian navy was prohibited from acquiring new battleships, submarines and aircraft carriers and it would be limited to a maximum force of 25,000 personnel. The Italian army was limited to a size of 185,000 personnel plus 65,000 Carabinieri for a maximum total of 250,000 personnel. The Italian Air force was limited to 200 fighters and reconnaissance aircraft plus 150 transport, air-rescue, training and liaison aircraft and was banned from owning and operating bomber aircraft. The number of air force personnel was limited to 25,000. Equally as severe were the political prohibitions including the banning fascist organizations ("whether political, military, or semi-military") in Italy (Treaty of Paris 1947).

Ongoing cold war tensions and its impact on Albanian-Italian relations

The Cold War polarisation of the world and especially Europe and the Balkans was polarising around the two sides of the political spectrum. Until 1949, Albania managed to remain unaligned neither with the West nor the East and yet managed to survive on the international stage. The hostile attitudes of neighbouring countries, as well as the Albanian economic situation, forced Albania to look initially to the Soviet Union for aid and support created by the termination of its alliance with Yugoslavia. Hoxha's views were in line with the USSR from 1949, and Soviet economic aid would play an important economic role for Albania.

In 1955, Albania was invited to join the Warsaw Treaty Organisation (known as the Warsaw Pact), where it was hoping that this security pact would provide it with security and military protection. Overall, it was clear to Hoxha that while it was reassuring to be a member of the Warsaw Pact, Albania felt excluded from discussions and decision-making so Albanian participation was more ceremonial (Hoxha 1983: 21).

After Stalin's death in March 1953 and the introduction of a new Soviet policy of "peaceful co-existence", Hoxha noted that ideological and political differences with the new USSR leader, Nikita Khrushchev, were now becoming unacceptable. Khrushchev's speech in February 1956 about the cult of Stalin was seen by Hoxha as a betrayal of the USSR and Stalin himself. Hoxha interpreted Khrushchev's position as a deviation from orthodox Marxism-Leninism, which he referred to as "revisionism" (Hoxha 1983: 25). Once this tension was internalised, Soviet economic aid to Albania began to decline, and by 1960, the possibility for Albania to secure long-term loans from the USSR was no longer an option.

Khrushchev's shift also affected Albanian domestic politics. In 1960, Hoxha's government survived the plot organised by the Soviet trained-Albanian Admiral Teme Sejko. Sejko was arrested and then sentenced to death. Further purges followed of high pro-Soviet members of the Party such as Liri Belishova and Koco Tashko. Moreover, the split between China and the Soviet Union in 1961, created a rupture in diplomatic relationships between Tirana and Moscow. Albania now shifted its attention and interest towards Mao's China. During this tumultuous period of the 1950s, Albania was finally accepted (December 1955) as a full member of the United Nations (UN) after years of insistence.

In 1956 Hoxha and Chinese leader Mao met in China, which was the initial first step toward a "steel-like unity" between the two countries (Tretiak 1962). As tensions were building up with the Soviet Union, Hoxha was moving closer to China and pleased to be able to secure Chinese aid and enjoy their special relationship. In Mao's speech, on 3 November 1966, Albania was claimed as the only Marxist-Leninist state in Europe stating:

> ... an attack on Albania will have to reckon with the great People's [Republic of] China. If the U.S. imperialists, the modern Soviet revisionists or any of their lackeys dare to touch Albania in the slightest, nothing lies ahead for them but a complete, shameful and memorable defeat (Hamm 1963: 43).

Post-war Italy and the undoing of decades of association with Albania

Post-War Europe was now deeply divided and engulfed in an ideological cold war. Italy was no exception and, in its desire to reconstruct its State, it had little choice but to do so with a powerful and large Italian Communist Party under the leadership of Palmiro Togliatti. Italy emerged from the war fragile with major war damage and obliged to pull together coalition governments with Communists involved in administering the new Italian state. Much of the connections with Albania would be dissolved and the new Italy had much to cope with itself in its new post-fascist political and economic framework.

Moreover, the ideological divisions of Europe and much of the world e would place Italy and Albania in contrast. There were still some historical sources of tension between Italy and Albania which included the treatment of Italians who remained in Albania after the Albanian Communist Party took power. During the Cold war, Italy entered into the minds of Albanians initially via radio and later on Albanian TV screens. However, as the Cold War intensified some felt that Italy had lost interest in Albania as relations declined to a very low ebb. This would change in 1949.

Diplomatic relations between Italy and Albania had still not been established. Remaining unresolved issues included Albania's request for Italy to repatriate war criminals to Albania as well as reparations suffered. The Italian side had the issue of the few remaining Italians to be repatriated back to Italy. Finally, in August 1949 diplomatic relations were established but this did not ease the tensions between the two countries and over the following years numerous clashes would occur between them. Throughout these moments of tension – the relations between the leadership of the PCI and the Albanian legation (Albanian Communist Party representation based in Italy) remained close. In October 1948 the PCI had been squeezed out of power and distanced from key State institutions. In Parliament the PCI would often attack the Christian Democratic government for its protection of Albanian war criminals and its hostility towards the new communist Albanian state. This strong relationship with the Italian Communist party lasted until Albania found itself no longer in tune with the Yugoslavia and later the USSR in the post Stalin period.

The Cold War and the Truman Doctrine – Italy and the tensions with Albania

From 1949 with the Marshall Plan alongside the new Cold War strategy of the Truman Doctrine inclusive of the establishment of NATO, Italy was seen at the centre of numerous plans to destabilise newly established Communist countries in its neighbourhood including that of Albania. Italy abandoned any pretence of "neutrality" and became one of the more fervent loyalists of the US-NATO objectives helped by the fact that in 1948 the Italian Communist Party had been removed from government in part with the help of covert and open campaigning by the US government to have the Communist Party removed from government.

1948 saw the first major crisis in the communist world post war with the split between Stalin and Tito. Albania took Stalin's side against Tito and did so removing pro Tito elements within the Albanian Communist Party. Albania's now close alliance with the USSR and its strategic focus on the Adriatic Coast captured the attention of US and British intelligence in Europe to such an extent that these two agencies put in place various actions including the use of former Albanian immigrants to destabilise and overturn the Albanian communist government. According to one scholar Italy was never in favour of the US and British approach of overthrowing Albania and preferred the form of status quo (Hoxha 2017). In August 1949 the then General Secretary for the Italian Ministry of Foreign Affairs, Vittorio Zoppi, during a meeting with US Secretary of State, Dean Acheson, indicated that Italy's view on Albania was that it should remain an independent nation. The US put the Italian position down still seeing Albania as an Italian protectorate.

In the early 1950s while Italy still considered Yugoslavia to be a strategic threat, Italy was invited to join the newly established Balkan Pact, combining Yugoslavia, Greece and Turkey – which had the intent of a pact against a possible invasion of the USSR in the Balkans. Italy declined although the US encouraged Italy to help put the USSR and Yugoslavia against each other. Italy annoyed at this suggestion made clear to the US that further encouragement of Yugoslavia would force Italy to re-examine its involvement in other Western military alliances.

In 1954 three important developments occurred which provided for greater ties between Italy and Albania. In 1954 a modest trade agreement was signed between the two nations and the two governments came to an understanding on reparations Italy the Italian occupation of Albania in the 1940s. With reparations agreed on, Italian civilians and military personnel still stuck in Albania would be allowed to return. Relations throughout the 1950s seemed stable until Italy allowed the US to install the Jupiter missiles on Italian territory. The installation of these missiles aroused anger from the USSR, Yugoslavia and Albania at the same time. Albania at the time, in protest against the Italian authorities, even threatened counter measures of installing Soviet missiles in Albania – though this never happened and Albania joining the Warsaw Pact in 1955, allowed for the USSR to install 12 modern submarines at its only Mediterranean base of Pashaliman, near Vlorë.

The other changes were on the horizon with relations between Albania and the Soviet Union coming to an end with a gradual deterioration of relations between 1955 and 1961 under Nikita Khrushchev. Concerning Albania in this dispute was the USSR coming closer to Yugoslavia, along with Khrushchev's "Secret Speech" denouncing Stalin thereby leading to a complete break in December 1961. Hoxha kept four Soviet submarines which infuriated the USSR threatening to attack the Albanian city of Vlorë, which never happened. This opened up major economic and commercial opportunities for Italy to trade with Albania – something which the US was concerned about seeing Italy's desire to replace the USSR as Albania's economic provider.

Albania's withdrawal from the Warsaw Pact and its alliance with China

With Albania in the Warsaw Pact, a fact related primarily to its strategic location in the Adriatic rather than her being a communist ally. The use of Albanian territory for the Soviet military raised concerns from across the Adriatic and especially from Italy. But as relations between Albania and the USSR had become very frosty and by 1961, a definitive break. Albania made it known that it had distanced itself from the Warsaw Pact (though not definitively leaving it until 1968). After the Soviet intervention in Czechoslovakia in 1968, Albania decided this was the moment to sever ties completely with the USSR. This intention aroused interest from Western powers and no less from Italy. Albania had already been moving closer to China from the time of the Sino-Soviet split in 1961 and at the same time feared a possible military attack from the USSR and/or Yugoslavia. Italy raised its voice of concern to this prospect and even indicated: "We will not remain indifferent if Albania is attacked" (taken from Smaci 2017:

158). On the other hand, Hoxha made clear that withdrawal from the Warsaw Pact would not change relations with Italy. Hoxha was quick to point out that Italy's concern was quite hypocritical given its membership of NATO and its attempts at the destabilisation of the Albanian government.

As China at the time was both consumed by its own internal dilemmas and conflicts and lacked the power and political importance it has today, Hoxha's decision to side with China attracted some attention in high places. Surprisingly given Albania's fragile existence it was surprising that it moved away from the protection of the Soviet Union. After 1968, for another decade, the entire Albanian economy, its health system, the industry, defence and foreign policy relied on China, and as a result, ties with the rest of the world were severed. However, the "steel-like unity" between Albania and China started to deteriorate in July 1971, after the Chinese premier Zhou Enlai agreed to meet with US President Richard Nixon during his visit to China. In 1973, Hoxha wrote in his diary (published in Reflections on China) that:

> Albania is no longer the "faithful, special friend" [of China] ... They are maintaining the economic agreements though with delays, but it is quite obvious that their [China's] "initial ardor" has died (Hoxha 1979: 41).

To create even more uncertainty, Tito's visit to Beijing in August-September 1977 convinced Hoxha that his hopes regarding the Chinese leadership were entirely dashed as he stated in his diary:

> To hell with them! We shall fight against all this trash, because we are Albanian Marxist-Leninists and on our correct course we shall always triumph! (Hoxha 1979: 107).

At this point Albania lost both Western and Eastern support, following Hoxha's unwise decision to pursue the complete isolation of his country from the world which proved disastrous for Albania's economy. By the time of the formal break with China in 1978, Albania had become isolated, with an economy close to collapse. From 1978 until the death of Hoxha in April 1985 are remembered as the toughest times for Albanian people under Hoxha.

Albania's domestic affairs during the Cold War

In 1946, rural Albanians were initially invited to join agricultural "cooperatives", a system that could offer them a higher possibility of automation in order to maximise their yields. Voluntary actions were sometimes followed by forced collectivisation, until private property was moved into the hands of the state. This was similar to the Soviet rural policy known as kolkhoz. However, it is clear that in some respects Albanian collectivisation went even deeper than that of the Soviet Union. By 1976 all cooperatives and farmland, resources, equipment and production in Albania had been nationalised.

While fostering growth in rural areas, the Albanian government kept urbanisation to a minimum through the development of certain industries. Often the Party decided who received government apartments and whether Albanians should live in cities, farms or cooperatives, as well as the place and type of work they should be employed in. The permission to have a TV at home was given by the Party, while Albania's only TV channel was strictly monitored by the State. The government considered the Ministry of Justice obsolete, which was eliminated in 1966 including abolishing the profession of lawyers as trials were completed without them. All open religious activities were deemed illegal and punishable.

Under the communist government in Albania, the average Albanian citizen faced restrictions on movement, on exit and entry into the country, and only a few were able to travel. Nevertheless, all members of these groups who could exit and enter Albania were strictly controlled by the regime, as were any figures who enjoyed external contacts or travel, such as writers and cultural celebrity figures. Although this category of Albanians had better pay and conditions, they were kept under closer scrutiny by the government. An example was the censorship on the Albanian writers. Even the work of the well-known Albanian writer, Ismail Kadare, was censured by Hoxha's regime. Any news and newspapers were scrutinised by the regime.

Voluntary activity was promoted and strongly supported by the communist government and most Albanians worked 6 days a week while Sundays were considered as societal "voluntary" days. Young Albanians – volunteers – built railways, roads and infrastructure. The large participation of young Albanians and especially the inclusion of women in these activities merits special attention. The Albanian social revolution was profound, but so too the political message. Propaganda about the new proletarian class included all levels of social strata such as children, youth, woman, farmers, blue and white-collar people. At a certain period of the year, Albanian intellectuals, students and workers would engage in forced military activity in what was called *zbor*. These compulsory activities were designed by the Party to support the country from attacks from "imperialism and revisionism". But the irony is that these activities and social organisation occurred in one of the poorest countries in Europe—a country with a weak economy challenged by peoples' basic needs. Another example was the voucher regime, which was the way the State sought to regulate and distribute the limited resources in the country. By 1989, education was free and compulsory for up until year eight, although further studies required a scholarship from the Party. As Vickers mentions:

> Although the country benefited from improved agriculture, industry, and in particular health and education, such initiatives were overshadowed by a horrific legacy of brutal repression... The Albanian people had been cowed into a fearful state of submission, which led them, like their country, to withdraw into themselves with their thoughts kept secret, paranoid and suspicious of all around them (Vickers 1995: 209).

Hoxha and his government established one of the strictest controls of its people and even more extreme than other Communist countries. By the end of the Cold War Hoxha's fortification fear and paranoia – its circa 800,000 bunkers would never be used against imperialism and revisionism. It was an example of the Socialist countries dedicating their scarce resources to the defence of their countries – a defence that would not even be tested.

The 1980s - Relations between Italy and Albania after the death of Hoxha

While there had been a strong relationship between Albania and Italy in pre-war times, much of this changed with Hoxha and the Albanian Socialist State. This changed to a certain extent with the death of Enver Hoxha in 1985. After the end of its relationship with China, trade relations between Albania and Italy grew, as shown on the table 4.1 below. Between 1977-1984, during Albania's "isolation", Albania traded more with Italy than any country in the world... and by a long shot. Italy's Under Secretary of State for Foreign Affairs, Bruno Corti, was the first senior Western official to visit Tirana after Hoxha's death. Before his departure for Albania, the Italian Foreign Ministry issued a statement stressing the importance of these discussions with Albania, adding that "this dialogue is of great interest to all the Western nations who can communicate with Albania through Italy" (Biberaj 1985: 42).

Table 4.1 Albanian trade with the West 1977 - 1984, $US in mill

Country/Year	1977	1980	1982	1984
Austria	9	14	17	13
Belgium	2	2	5	-
France	8	14	35	40
West Germany	21	29	53	29
Greece	14	39	25	-
Italy	**33**	**65**	**74**	**49**
Japan	5	2	14	7
Netherlands	11	9	12	11
Norway	-	-	2	1
Spain	-	3	12	10
Sweden	5	9	9	14
Turkey	3	14	3	-
UK	-	3	8	8
USA	9	19	20	12

Source: Adopted from Biberaj 1985: 46

Of all the countries of the West, Italy was always a first port of call for Albania. When the two countries met during a visit to Rome in December 1984, the Albanian First Deputy Foreign Minister Sokrat Plaka, declared that Albania "is seeking partners in the West, and is looking to Italy in particular in view of the social and cultural ties between the two countries" (Biberaj 1985: 42). Some months earlier, in December 1983, a maritime line linking the ports of Durrës and Trieste was established and the two nations also signed a long-term trade agreement by which Italy would provide Albania with substantial industrial technology in return for raw materials (Biberaj 1985). The importance that Albania attached to the further strengthening of its relations with Italy became particularly evident in May 1985, when Albanian Prime Minister, Adil Carcani sent a more sincere message to the Italian Prime Minister Bettino Craxi, expressing a desire for better cooperation between the two countries (Biberaj 1985).

To the surprise of Albania and other nations, the incident in mid-1985, where Prime Minister Craxi found himself facing off US President Reagan over international jurisdiction in relation to the Achille Lauro incident involving Palestinian terrorists and the killing of a Jewish passenger on board the Achille Lauro. Craxi decided to block the US administration from involvement in the Achille Lauro events. The US administration was furious creating significant distrust with the US ally. This incident did not escape international attention and certainly not Albania which saw this as an act of defiance by Italy against the US.

Following the death of Hoxha in 1985, Ramiz Alia (who survived Hoxha's political purges), emerged as the First Secretary of Albania's Socialist Party [the new name of Labour Party of Albania (PLA)]. Albania during this period was looking to establish relations with both East and West and in August 1987, it resumed diplomatic relations with Greece, now an indication of more openness in Albania's foreign policy.

In 1988, after a historic meeting of the Albanian foreign minister Reis Malile with the foreign ministers of Yugoslavia, Bulgaria, Greece, Turkey and Romania in Belgrade, Ramiz Alia—welcomed the Turkish foreign minister Mesut Yilmaz to Tirana (Tase 2014). The visit was returned in 1990 by an Albanian delegation to Turkey. During the isolation period of Albania, trade with Turkey was insignificant compare to that of Italy. The end of Hoxha's regime in Albania ushered a new era of continuous and uninterrupted relations between Turkey and Albania. At the end of the Cold War, Albania's economic needs were enormous, and Turkish authorities provided primarily lip service for their "little sister", Albania. Only the Albanian-Italian minority, the Arbëresh, maintained ties with the other side of the Adriatic, mainly for its own genealogical purposes, by participating in common cultural initiatives such as congresses on the Albanian language.

The fall of the Berlin Wall and the end of the Soviet Union

Cracks were appearing in Eastern Europe long before the fall of the Berlin Wall and the end of Soviet Union in 1991. The mid 1970s saw the small window of détente come to an end and a return to the rekindling of the Cold War tensions reminiscent of the 1950s. US President Carter championed the 'Human Rights' crusade against the Soviet Union in 1977 and a year later, the Cold War Pope John Paul II became the new pontiff in the Vatican. Tension between the Cold War powers took a turn for the worse in late December 1979, when the Soviet Union intervened in Afghanistan, an action which President Carter characterized as 'the greatest threat to peace since the WWII'. Carter called for the postponement of the SALT-II nuclear weapons treaty and recalled the U.S. ambassador to the Soviet Union. During the next period a number of other significant changes raised the stakes in the Cold War. In 1980 Ronald Reagan capitalized on public fear of Soviet assertiveness and won the presidency from Jimmy Carter. The extreme tension internationally became visible with retaliatory measures such as the missile program deployment in Europe and tensions relating to issues in Afghanistan and Poland.

Soviet intelligence services went on alert in 1981 to watch for US preparations for launching a surprise nuclear attack against the USSR and its allies. A new Soviet intelligence collection program, known by the acronym RYAN, to monitor indications and provide early warning of US intentions, accompanied this alert. Two years later a major war scare erupted in the USSR. Cold War rhetoric intensified in the early years of the Reagan Administration. President Reagan called the Soviet Union an 'evil empire' in March 1983. In the same month of March, Reagan announced plans to proceed with a space-based missile defence that became known as 'Star Wars'. Despite heavy criticism, Reagan pushed ahead with research and development of the multi-billion-dollar project. In 1986 the Chernobyl nuclear power station reactor core fuel exploded, sending a radioactive cloud containing some 50 million curies of radiation around Europe and the world. Large peace movements mobilised throughout the mid and late 1980s as the missile deployment in Europe from both the US and the USSR only exacerbated relations between the two powers. In the early 1980s the USSR had seen as spate of change of leadership of the elders. When Brezhnev died in 1982, he left the Soviet economy in deep trouble. In the early 1980s the Politburo was dominated by old men, and they were overwhelmingly Russian. Yury Andropov and then Konstantin Chernenko led the country from 1982 until 1985, but their administrations failed to address critical problems.

The arrival of Mikhail Gorbachev in 1985 provided a new lease of life in the USSR leadership but unwittingly also opened cracks in the Soviet leadership and in the Soviet Union itself. Under Gorbachev's proposed reforms for the Soviet Union and his conciliatory approach towards the West, opened the government to attacks from the old guard. Some of the reformist policies in the Soviet Union fuelled opposition movements to the Communist governments in the Soviet hemisphere. When Gorbachev visited East Berlin in October 1989 (ironically to celebrate the 40th anniversary of the East German state), his mere presence encouraged demonstrators to call for his help chanting: 'Gorby! Gorby! Help us!'. Only weeks later, the Berlin Wall came down and by May 1990, Gorbachev agreed that Germans had the right to decide their own future and German reunification received Soviet endorsement for the first time since 1945.

With his call for *perestroika* ("restructuring"), Gorbachev was of the view that the basic economic structure of the USSR was sound in need of only reforms. He thus pursued an economic policy that aimed to increase economic growth while increasing capital investment. His goal was quite simple: to bring the Soviet Union up to par economically with the West. Two years later, however, Gorbachev concluded that deeper structural changes were necessary. In 1987–88 he pushed through reforms that went someway to the creation of a semi-free market system. The consequences of this form of a semi-mixed economy with the contradictions of the reforms themselves brought economic chaos to the country and unpopularity to Gorbachev. Despite many urging Gorbachev to move even more vigorously to a fully-fledged market economy, Gorbachev, never intended to make that jump not even to a mixed economy.

Gorbachev launched *glasnost* ("openness") as the second vital plank of his reform efforts. He believed that the opening up of the political system—essentially, democratizing it—was the only way to overcome inertia in the political and bureaucratic apparatus, which had a big interest in maintaining the status quo. *Glasnost* also allowed the media more freedom of expression, and editorials complaining of depressed conditions and of the government's inability to correct them began to appear.

The collapse of Soviet Communism led to dislocation of the Soviet Union, sapped by an ideological, political and economic crisis. This in turn precipitated the break-up of the Federation. One after another the Soviet Socialist Republics (SSRs) proclaimed their national sovereignty in the summer of 1991. In December of the same year, some of these republics, which had become independent, redefined their respective links by creating the Commonwealth of Independent States (CIS). With Boris Yeltsin ready to assume power, the end of the Soviet Union was assured and the openness of the former CPSU to hand over political power to "democrats". One of the first pieces of legislation of the new Russia was the banning of the Communist Party! The Soviet Union exhausted and economically bankrupt, imploded, and contrary to CIA intelligence expectations that collapse would occur from an open conflict with the West. This did not happen. The West won a significant victory without a shot being fired.

Prelude to the destruction of Yugoslavia

Tito's death in 1980 signalled trouble for the Yugoslavian federation and the Balkans in general. The vacuum created by Tito's disappearance was filled by new leaders – the Slovenian Milan Kučan and the Serbian Slobodan Milošević. By late 1980s the political rivalry between the republics was transformed into ethnic rivalry. The fall of the Berlin Wall in 1989 and the subsequent collapse of the Soviet Union and its Eastern European allies in 1990/91 had a direct effect on Yugoslavian unity. The Yugoslav federal leadership in the face of serious economic crisis and without Tito to look to, saw its leadership, the League of Yugoslavian Communists lose their political control and no longer being able to hold Yugoslavia together.

Despite the optimism of Yugoslav's last Prime Minister, Ante Marković to reform Yugoslavia, he will be remembered as powerless in face of open rebellion from the main three republics, Serbia, Slovenia and Croatia. Nationalists from each territory predominantly won the first elections that were held in Yugoslavia since 1945. Serbian nationalism launched a separatist drive but the real intention of Milošević was to take over the Yugoslav federation (Silber and Little 1997: 70). Slovenia did not want to follow the same rules as other republics and Croatia was protective of its decision to keep its foreign currency due to its dependency on tourism. Croatia was silent after Tito's crushing of the Maspuk-communists in 1971 and dismantling of Croatia's cultural organisation, Matica Hrvatska due to its nationalistic platform against Serbs. By late 1980's Croats were anxiously seeing the growth of new Serbian nationalistic leaders such as Milošević. It is arguable that the anti-Serbian sentiment drove Croatian migrants to reach out again for the Ustasha movement, which sympathised and collaborated with the Nazi's during the Second World War. It also helped Croatia to leave behind the byzantine legacy and bolster their identity as Westerners associated with Catholicism and with little in common with Serbs. Nonetheless, it was not until 1989 the Croatian biggest nationalist group was consolidated under controversial general Franjo Tudjman. Following the lead of Slovenia, Croatia also intended separation from Yugoslavia. Tudjman who was no less nationalistic than Milošević, had been part of the Maspuk purges in 1970's and 1980's and as a winner of elections in 1990, would serve as the first President of Croatia.

Serbian leadership was hoping that religious affiliation of Muslims of Bosnia and Herzegovina and Kosovar Albanians would boost their loyalty to Yugoslavia rather than follow the Catholic Slovenes and Croats. On the basis of this assumption, Milošević sought to convince the Muslim leadership to stay within Yugoslavia while having talks with Tudjman about the separation of Yugoslavia (Judah 2009: 198). This approach with both Bosnian Muslims and Kosovar-Albanians failed and moreover reversing Kosovo's regional autonomy status in 1989 created further unrest. The only option was now for him to expand on his talks with Tudjman to insist on a safe passage to Serbs who were living in Bosnia-Herzegovina. Tensions remained high across Yugoslavia and Bosnia saw more trouble when the Croatian flag flew in Western Herzegovina and the Muslim leadership also wanted their own separation while in Serbia the population began demonstrating its own loyalty to its leadership. Under pressure from Germany, the EU recognised Slovenia and Croatia in 1992 while Bosnia began slipping towards civil war. The trouble in Sarajevo was obvious after Muslim-Bosniaks shoutings "Allahu Akhbar" at places where the "U" symbol of the Ustasha Croats and Serb Chetniks were present. What followed was ethnic clashes and the end of Yugoslavia alongside the genocide that took place in Srebrenica, a tragic repetition of what happened at the end of the previous century.

Kosovar Albanians as part of the Yugoslavian federation

Ethnic Albanians living in Macedonia, Montenegro and Serbia found themselves to be part of Yugoslavia after WWII since their territories were left out of Albania in 1913. The biggest percentage and number of Albanian speaking population left outside of the Albania proper lived in Kosovo – a territory that was incorporated within Yugoslavia and later Serbia. Kosovar Albanians as well as other Albanians within the Federation did not have the same rights as other ethnic compositions such as Serbs, Croats, Montenegrin and Macedonians. In 1968 Kosovar Albanian students took streets of Pristina demanding their rights to be equal as other Yugoslavian citizens. They demanded an autonomous status within the federation, education and establishment of at least one University where they can learn in Albanian language. The right to freely expose the Albanian national flag was also a request. Except the Albanian national flag, Tito granted other requests and Kosovo upgraded its status from region to a province of Yugoslavia. Constitutional changes in 1974 recognised the composition of Yugoslavia by 8 units where Kosovo and Vojvodina were equally considered the additional two autonomous units. These constitutional changes increased the discontent of Serbs as both these provinces were considered part of Serbia. After Tito's death, Kosovar-Albanian protests ignited again in 1981 as the anti-Albanian sentiment increased in Serbia. This was a time when media and other circles of academics in Serbia conducted a real propaganda campaign against Albanians (Malcolm 1999: 338). An example was in 1986 when the Serbian Academy of Sciences and Arts came up with a memorandum, arguing that Serbs of Kosovo were facing 'genocide' at the hands of Albanian majority and called on Serbia to reassert its authority over the province. This provided an ideal chance for Milošević to enhance his political career (Ker-Lindsay 2009: 10). The developments of the 1980s, from Kosovo expanded to other parts of Yugoslavia where Serbs were living in minority. Thus, Milošević used the "victimisation" of Serbs as the main driving force to drag the Federation towards a one-party system dominated by Serbs. Milošević's famous speech in 1987 during demonstrations in Kosovo where he claimed that 'no one would be able to beat Serbs', transformed him into a national hero (Malcolm 1999: 342). It was now easy for him to rise to the highest levels of the Serbian League of Communists, even overthrowing the then president of the party and his mentor, Stambolic.

The abolishment of the autonomy for Kosovo in March 1989 was seen with fear and scepticism from other republics and it accelerated the disintegration of Yugoslavia. Milošević's followed with his speech in June 1989 in North Kosovo celebrating the battle of Kosovo Polje in 1389, which infuriated Kosovar-Albanians. It all culminated in December 1989 with the establishment of the Kosovar-Albanian movement, the Democratic League of Kosovo (LDK), which was now a political entity that was legally registered in the new constitution.

The start of the disintegration of Yugoslavia and the end of "Socialist" Albania

The bad economic situation of Yugoslavia was accompanied by political and ethnic crushes during the 1990's. Following the free elections in 1990, Croatians led by Tudjman did not hide their separatist sentiment. Serbian government on the other hand started to organise and manipulate Croatian Serbs in Knin by allowing them to access weapons from a police station so that the Croatian Serbs could mount a successful revolt against the Croatian government. Croatian Serbs blocked the roads that linked to Dalmatia in what is known as "log revolution", which damaged seriously Croatian tourism. Milošević sent a Serbian Army officer and the Federal Interior Minister, Petar Gracanin to support the revolt and demanded Croatian government to stop sending police forces against Serbs (Silber and Little 1997: 100). Instead, the Croatian government sent military helicopters to stop the revolt, but soon the Federal Army jets forced Croatian helicopters and police forces to return to their Zagreb base. After this episode, it did become clear that Milošević held the power of what was once Yugoslavian People's Army. In October, Croatian representative Stjepan Mesic joined Slovenia, Bosnia and Herzegovina and Macedonian counterparts to oppose the state of emergency, which would have given Yugoslav People's Army to place the martial law. The majority (88.5%) of Slovenian people voted pro Independence in their December 1990 referendum. It was not a surprise that 99.25 per cent of Croatians followed suit in a similar referendum in May 1991. Yugoslavia had now started to disintegrate, and the entire Western Balkan political landscape was about to change.

Events of 1989 were also felt in Albania. The Albanian mass exodus to foreign Embassies in July 1989 found the Albanian government unprepared for this turn of events. News from Berlin and the collapse of the USSR was penetrating through to Albanians through Italian, Greek and Yugoslav television. The student and popular revolt of discontent people was mounting, and the situation was fast turning out of control for the Alia government. After meeting with some intellectual figures in August, Alia was forced to accept the concept of 'pluralism' in November 1990. Albanian students and intellectuals formed their own party the Democratic Party (PD) in December 1990, marking a new era in Albania. PD won the first free elections in March 1991, but the economic situation was disastrous. The arrival of some form of parliamentary democracy was one thing, the state of the Albanian economy was another. Crisis was looming.

Photo 7: Italian Occupation in Albania according to La Domenica del Corriere, 1919
License: Public domain, Wikipedia Commons.

Photo 8: Delegates of the Congress of Lushnje in January 1920.
License: Public domain, Wikipedia Commons.

Photo 9: Italian soldiers passing Albanians, 7 April 1939
License: Public domain, Wikipedia Commons.

Photo 10: Italian invasion of Albania 13 April 1939.
Source: Varni A., 2016, *La storia nelle prime pagine del Corriere della Sera*, Rizzoli Libri SpA, Milano, p. 206.

Photo 11: King Zog I and the Italian Minister Galeazzo Ciano in 1937
License: Public domain, Wikipedia Commons.

Albania and the Italian "partner"

Photo 12: Benito Mussolini 1930
License: Public domain, Wikipedia Commons.

Photo 13: Portrait of a young Enver Hoxha during the war, 1940
License: Public domain, Wikipedia Commons.

Photo 14: Musine Kokalari, c.1925-9, License: Public domain, Wikipedia Commons.

Photo 15: Professor Isuf Luzaj
Licence: Isuf Luzaj Official Website.

5

Western Balkans move towards Europe – Italian interest in Albania subsides

With the fall of the Berlin Wall in November 1989 little did we expect that the entire Central and Eastern European sphere of communist countries would follow with the ultimate collapse of the Soviet Union in 1991. On its heels, and not unexpectedly was the disintegration of Yugoslavia which not only ceased to exist but spiralled into bloody ethnic reprisals and cleansing of a brutality not seen in decades. In an equally consequential and chaotic manner, though less bloody, Albania had a few years earlier experienced the end of the Hoxha period and in 1991 it saw the end of its communist legacy. Albania had little to look forward to except political wilderness and economic collapse.

The early years of the 1990s in Italy were just as historic and turbulent, as Italy's deep political crisis emerged through the 1992 anti-corruption campaign. What became evident not only by its timing, was how the corruption revelations were in part as result of the end of the Cold War and its Italian manifestations. The early 1990s was also the time for Italy's impending approval of the Maastricht Treaty committing Italy to internal economic reforms which had eluded it for decades. Italy, along with other member states would lose its monetary and currency "parachute" which it had used to escape its international loss of competitiveness over many years. Like all new contenders for the single currency in Europe, the loss of its currency and financial independence would not be digested easily but it was seen as a necessity to not be left behind in Europe. With these political distractions, Italy's ability to remain focused on what was happening nearby in the Balkans as it unravelled, was a more difficult task. At the same time, this new era with the Cold War behind it, including its domestic repercussions of the same (e.g., the dissolution of the Italian Communist Party), opened for Italy, the prospect of playing a more assertive role in foreign policy.

The end of the Cold War and the collapse of the Soviet Union - effects on Italy

Only three weeks after the fall of the Berlin Wall, Mikhail Gorbachev visited Italy, the first ever visit by a Soviet Communist Party General Secretary. During this visit, besides giving the then leader of the Italian Communist Party, Achille Occhetto support for his efforts to reform his party, Gorbachev also reaffirmed the scaling down of the Cold War and stated: 'The Cold War has ended, or is ending...not because there are victors and vanquished, but precisely because there are neither' (Bufacchi and Burgess 2001: 16). Gorbachev had re-assured the Italian government that the end of the Cold War would produce a new era of international relations, an era in which probably no one knew its significance. Gorbachev took on key stumbling blocks of the Cold War - the reunification of Germany, the dissolution of the Warsaw Pact, withdrawal from Afghanistan, nuclear and conventional arms control, and, most significantly in 1991, the U.S.-led effort to liberate Kuwait in Operation Desert Storm. But in no way had Gorbachev imagined that this would mean the breakup of the Soviet Union which he blamed on power hungry and determined individuals such as Boris Yeltsin. It says much for Gorbachev's naivety for the future and the desire of other leaders of the USSR to see its downfall. The period was defined by confusion and fear rather than any surefooted analysis and few saw this collapse of the USSR coming on.

Back in Italy, the hitherto uneventful Presidency of Francesco Cossiga was about to change again in a post-Cold War environment. Clearly feeling that times allowed for these indiscretions, Cossiga revealed the existence of a secret NATO organization operating on Italian territory during the post-war period. This revelation was confirmed by another former Prime Minister, Andreotti, in October 1990, who admitted the existence of this same clandestine secret structure called 'Stay Behind' codenamed Gladio. This structure had been set up and formalized with the CIA in 1956, with the aim of confronting a potential Warsaw Pact invasion. While many of the former Christian Democratic leaders denied the existence of such a structure, these revelations explained many things - not least the involvement of the US/NATO in peacetime conditions to provide leadership in repelling any possible move towards government by the Italian Communists, in the event they gained electoral success. It also confirmed that covert anti-communist activities had been taking place uninterruptedly in the aftermath of the Second World War and were only just becoming public knowledge. The revelations however also acknowledged that the fear of the Cold War settings was now a thing of the past and informing the public of what actually had happened was now possible.

With the collapse of East and Central Europe, and alongside this, the disintegration of the Balkans, the question of Albania presented itself starkly given Italy's special relationship with this country. Yet Italy's policy towards Albania contained two almost conflicting approaches. While Italy was aware that it had the first option on Albania from a Western perspective as the nation with the greatest connection and links to Albania, it was also the country which would require the greatest investment from a security dimension – something Italy did not relish. The nature of Albania, its poverty and poor prospects was not what Italy had bargained for. In contrast to Albanian hopes, the nation of greater interest for Italy was Serbia although other powerful neighbours were also taking an interest.

The Italian reaction to the fall of Albania and Operation Pelican

In late 1989 the Andreotti government had just embarked on a more incisive dialogue and relationship with Yugoslavia through a so-called Adriatic Initiative. As an afterthought, Italy also sought out Albanian inclusion in this initiative. Its aim was to provide a platform for greater exchange and collaboration between Yugoslavia and the European Economic Community as well as addressing the complex Kosovo question. Hesitant at first, Albania in November 1989, through its Ambassador in Rome, Bashkim Dino, informed Italian Foreign Affairs that Albania was ready to join the 'Adriatic initiative' in order to strengthen relations with its neighbours. While the intentions were good, the collapse of Albania only months later would sink the optimism that this initiative had encouraged.

As Eastern European communist governments fell in 1990-91, and much of the Balkans was hurtled into ethnic war, Albania initially appeared to be an exception. With Ramiz Alia at the helm, the Albanian Labour Party, for a while managed to hold onto power in this turbulent period. But months later, Albania descended into its first serious moment of political turmoil with many Albanians fleeing the country along with many seeking refuge in foreign embassies. In Italy's case there was an estimated 800 Albanians huddled in its Embassy in Tirana. The case that however caught the most attention was the Popa Case – where six brothers from the same family sought refugee status in the Italian Embassy. The Albanian authorities were determined to arrest these siblings and for some time tension ensued between Albania and Italy. It was an impasse which seemed to have little sign of ending until May 1990 when the Alia government eventually permitted the release of the Popa family allowing them to travel to Italy. From that moment onwards, the Albanian government ceased to put up resistance to Albanians leaving the country.

Over the following 12 months greater numbers of Albanians fled the country amidst the deeper levels of political and economic crisis. This included many seeking entry into Italy catching the Italian border police and government by surprise. Some 28,000 set out for Italy by boat simply overwhelming the Italian authorities with these arrivals. The Albanian government in these months teetered from one crisis to another producing revolving door governments. The country was facing an abyss and the economy was in free fall collapse and the people were facing food shortages. Italian aid arrived soon after but made little difference to the sufferance felt by the populace.

When Albania began facing its ultimate decline, the traditional approach Italy had with its former protectorate had changed significantly. The appetite to see Albania as its modest colony and foothold in the Balkans had become muted and significantly downplayed. What was left of Albania in 1990-91 was less attractive than what it might have been during and immediately after World War Two. An indicative view of the changed emotions was provided by these observers:

> Eventually, not only Italian memory of colonialism in Albania but the neighbouring country itself gradually disappeared from Italian collective representations. Only the Albanian-Italian minority, the Arbëresh, kept hold of some ties with the other side of the Adriatic, mainly for its own genealogical purposes, by participating in common cultural initiatives such as congresses on the Albanian language. In fact, by the time of the regime change in Albania in 1991, Italian public opinion had almost completely forgotten the neighbouring country (Chiodi & Devole 2006: 5).

At first the Italians conveyed a certain empathy for the arriving Albanians, but this did not last long. Ironically in March 1990, after years of debate and independently of the mass arrivals from Albania, Italy introduced one of the more stringent migration laws in its history known as the Martelli Law to deal with "illegal immigration". The then Primer Minister Andreotti flippantly remarked in view of the impending arrival of thousands of desperate Albanian immigrants that "each Italian adapt an Albanian. If enough Italians did this, there would no longer be a refugee problem"! (Woods 1992: 186). Over time this flippant remark would highlight how out of touch and unprepared the Italian authorities were of this uninterrupted human flow from Albania.

It was clear that Italy was unable to cater for the thousands of Albanians entering Italy as immigrants. In order to stem this flow from Albania, Italy felt it needed to revise its approach and reverted towards helping the political and economic stabilisation in Albania. As part of this changed approach Italy in August 1991 now pursued: 1. Immediate repatriation of refugees; 2. Tight control of the coastline; 3. New immediate shipments of food aid to Albania and; 4. Involvement of the European Community in resolving the Albanian crisis.

The collapse of Albania in 1991, different from its neighbours in the former Yugoslavia was more chaotic than bloody. Albanians, despite their isolation, were aware of the Fall of the Berlin Wall and the collapse of Communism in Eastern Europe. While the fall of the Communist government was a peaceful event in Albania, the new elections in March 1991 would neither bring clarity or recovery. Italy, while about to face the effects of the Albanian collapse, was at the time more concerned by the international tensions which had surfaced over the Gulf War which for the first time since the end of the Second World War, saw Italian forces involved in armed conflict. Other international concerns included the re-unification of Germany, the negotiations which would lead to the Maastricht Treaty, and the development of the Yugoslav situation. One commentator aptly summarised the immediate consequences for Italy on the eve of the Albanian collapse:

> In 1991 the definitive collapse of the Albanian Communist regime caused a phenomenon of mass emigration which imposed on both the Italian political leadership and public opinion the need to face the dramatic consequences of the fall of Communism in this Balkan country and to establish a new

policy towards a neighbour which had been almost completely ignored for about forty-five years. Albania had long been a traditional focus of Italy's foreign policy (Varsori 2012: 616).

After the exodus of some 28,000 Albanians crossing the Adriatic Sea in mid-summer of 1991, a further 21,000 immigrants made their way across the sea towards the Italian peninsular. A concerned Italy began to see large numbers building up in southern cities especially in the Apulia region and empathy soon turned into questions of public order. While receptive at first, Italy now resorted to brutal administrative solutions including gathering thousands of Albanian refugees and holding them in football stadiums left in the sun without proper facilities in the heat of Italy's hot August. Repatriations back to Albania began and, in a few months, some 28,000 Albanians were sent home. What defined the Italian response more generally would come with Operation Pelican which not only offered aid and assistance to Albanians but also ensured they would not return to Italy.

Operation Pelican

A new foreign policy towards Albania was imperative and a swift response from Italian authorities was emerging in its bid to check this uncontrolled exodus. The Italian operation "Pellicano", which commenced in September 1991 and completed in December 1993 took on a humanitarian emergency. The Italian Ministry of Defence website stated:

> The Italian Government decided to send the humanitarian aid to Albania, in order to discourage more migration and return those migrants that illegally entered Italy (*Ministero della Difesa*, ND).

Soon after the establishment of diplomatic relations between Albania and the European Economic Community in June 1991, Operation Pelican was launched in October 1991, involving the provision of emergency aid, mainly food and medicine. It employed 5,000 Italian soldiers who distributed 300,000 tons of food and emergency aid. What was unique about this mission was the absence of civil conflict between Albanians, either of an ethnic or religious kind. People were starving and the programme focused on feeding the population. The majority of Italian soldiers in Albania involved in the operation were unarmed and operated primarily as an aid provider. The Italian military aid covered the entire country and they were in some cases the first foreigners ever to have been in touch with locals.

As Albania moved towards some level of stability Italy began to take a greater interest economically and especially from an investment standpoint. Besides being the largest donor of foreign aid at the time of the 1991 Albanian collapse, 75 per cent of all foreign capital in Albania was Italian. ENI, the Italian hydrocarbon monolith signed an agreement with Tirana to exploit Albania's energy resources. Moreover, Italy promised investment in infrastructure, highways, rail and the Durrës Harbour and Italy began advocating for Albania to have stronger relations with the European community. In addition, the Italian government was wary of any view which encouraged the Yugoslav disintegration through the use of force. By early January 1992 in an assessment of its support to Albania, Italy acknowledged its coastal patrols, tons of food aid as well as 700 military personnel located in two Albanian towns Vlorë and Durrës which would continue under the Operation Pelican.

Italy IFOR[1] and Joint Endeavour

The disintegration of Yugoslavia and the ethnic wars that had ensued was such that in August 1995 the US and its NATO allies began a campaign of air-strikes against the Bosnian Serbs. This combined with a successful Muslim-Croat military offensive forced the Bosnian

---

1   IFOR – NATO led implementation force.

Serbs to agree to a negotiated settlement in Dayton, Ohio in November 1995. As a result, in December 1995 Italy contributed a brigade to IFOR, the NATO operation within a UN authorized peace-keeping operation (IFOR), which deployed troops to Sarajevo and in Bosnia-Herzegovina. Not only did Italy join but it also allowed the use of its bases for the air-strikes. Italy's felt obliged to contribute to a peace mission given the proximity of its borders to the former Yugoslavia and as a way to be included in the Contact Group of leading countries on the Balkans.

IFOR's primary mission was to implement the peace agreement which included the cessation of hostilities and to separate the armed forces of the Bosnian-Croat Federation and the Republika Srpska. It also included the transfer territory between the two entities, to move their forces and heavy weapons into safe sites and to create a secure environment for the UN High Representative and other organisations responsible for implementing the civil aspects of the peace agreement. These tasks required patrolling a separation zone along the 1,400km-long inter-entity boundary line and establishing and monitoring over 800 sites containing heavy weapons and other forces. In carrying out these tasks, IFOR opened 2,500km of roads, repaired or replaced over 60 bridges, and freed up Sarajevo airport and the railway system.

Missing Albanian gold: The intrigue comes to an end

In 1996 Albania was finally compensated for an alleged gold theft from the Albanian central bank during the Second World War. The dispute over the return of 1.5 tons of gold held by the Bank of England and taken from the collapsed Nazi regime at the end of the Second World War was finally concluded and agreed by all parties involved in the negotiation. The former Allies agreed that monetary gold — referring mostly to marked central bank reserves — looted by Germany and recovered by Allied forces at the end of the Second World War would be pooled and distributed to claimant countries in proportion to their losses. The Tripartite Commission for the Restitution of Monetary Gold was dissolved after distributing the remaining 5.5 tons, held as a contingency reserve, among the nine other claimant countries: Austria, Belgium, Greece, Italy, Luxembourg, the Netherlands, Poland and former Czechoslovakia and Yugoslavia. A final settlement was delayed because Britain, the United States, Italy and Albania presented conflicting claims to the gold claims.

The Albanian gold, originally seized by German troops from the Bank of Italy in Rome in 1943, had been held for the previous 50 years by the Allies. The gold, which Allied forces recovered in Germany after the Nazi defeat, was held in France. The UK claim for the gold was in relation to the compensation for the destruction of a British warship by Albanian mines in the Strait of Corfu in 1946 when Albania illegally planting mines in the strait in 1946, after the end of the war. Britain took its case to the International Court at The Hague, which found Tirana responsible for the mining incident, in which 44 British troops were killed. The communist government, in power in Tirana at the time of the incident, refused to accept the ruling. With the fall of communism in Albania in 1991, negotiations to recover the gold resumed, and the agreement to return half of the gold was signed after the Tirana government accepted The Hague ruling.

Political instability and quasi civil war – the renewed Albanian crisis of 1997

On the back of the questionable 1996 election results in Albania which saw Sali Berisha re-elected, political conditions deteriorated sending Albania into political and economic chaos. Moreover, to make matters worse, the 1997 financial pyramid scheme collapse which saw people's savings of over $US1 billion go up in smoke in government supported Pyramid schemes only added fuel to the already discredited government.

Reactions and protests to this crisis brought a breakdown in order with some cities occupied by rebels especially in the south, verging towards a civil war. Media outlets in Albania and outside reported over 2,000 deaths as a result of the disorder and the same year the government lost control of areas of the country (Jarvis 2000: 1). In the absence of a credible government authority, armed gangs often associated with political parties, took control of entire areas such as the city of Vlorë. Examples of this include Gazmend Braka establishing the Gaxhai's gang, supported by Berisha's Democratic Party while Myrteza Caushi established the Zani gang, that served the Socialist Party. Soon these gangs organised armed resistance against the government despite orders from the government to have them put down. However, this "Robin Hood" style of gang warfare was just the beginning and it soon escalated into other criminal activities and against each other.

Making matters worse was the incident involving two Albanian air force pilots, who landed their MIG17 at the Italian airbase of Galattina (Lecce) in March 1997. The MIG17 was headed for Southern Albania and according to pilots, they were ordered to bomb the Mifoli bridge – the only road connection of Vlorë region with Tirana. Albanians from the South considered this act as a declaration of war by the government and revolts escalated. A sort of rivalry between those in the North, loyal to Berisha versus the "socialist" South. As a result, many military depots in Albania were ransacked plunging the country into total chaos. It is estimated that at the time, the Albanian population which numbered less than three million, possessed more than a million guns (*The Irish Times* 1998).

With the Albanian government legitimacy in tatters, it signalled to neighbours especially Serbia and Greece, that opportunities for territorial grab were available. The "ghost" of North-Epirus was again resurrected with the Greek flag flown in protest in Sarandë, Delvinë and Gjirokastër in South Albania while in the North of the country there was a real danger of a Serbian invasion (Limaj 2012: 106-8). When Serbia bombed Albanian villages on the border bringing further turmoil to Albania and provoking yet another political crisis for the new provisional government led by Bashkim Fino. Both Braka and Caushi were arrested and sentenced to life imprisonment. After the fall of the communist government in Albania and mass exodus to Italy in 1991, this unrest degenerated into a quasi-civil war, and witnessed some of Albania's darkest days of the post-Cold War.

Italy's response to the new crisis in 1997 – Operation Alba

Beginning in early 1997, the Albanian government lost control of much of its country, culminating in the desertion of many police and military units and the looting of their armouries. The resulting chaos caused several countries to autonomously evacuate their nationals from Albania, which prompted concerns about the fate of others. With the Albanian state and economy crippled, Italy would become the logical location for the wave of refugees, and initially some 20,000 arrived in southern Italy with authorities totally unprepared for these arrivals. In March 1997, Italy appealed to the EU to develop a coordinated community plan to deal with these refugees. The EU was in no mood to do anything but lip service and the question of sending in peacekeeping troops was all but blocked by the UK and Germany especially.

In 1997, the new Italian government led by Romano Prodi, was administered by a broader and less manageable centre-left coalition government. Sentiment for sending Italian troops in this new mission (Operation Alba) while seen positively by the majority of the centre left, failed to receive support from the centre right led by Silvio Berlusconi. Eventually a recompacted coalition was required to achieve the majority support to send in Italian troops into Albania. Operation

Alba became a multinational peacekeeping force led by Italy, intended to help the Albanian government restore law and order during the de facto Albanian Civil War. The UN Security Council requested the establishment of an operation that would stabilize the situation. Italy assumed responsibility for the stop-gap mission as Operation Alba, the first armed multinational Italian-led Mission since World War II. The eleven nations that participated in this operation were Austria, Belgium, Denmark, France, Greece, Italy, Portugal, Romania, Slovenia, Spain and Turkey. The Italian led military mission was seen favourably by the European neighbours and it was obvious that Italy had the greatest motivation to be involved given the threat of a flood of refugees onto its territory. Italy however also had historic reasons for the leadership role like the Operation Pelican in 1991 which was seen with some favour by Albanians.

However, the tensions with Italy emerged almost overnight by the collision between the Albanian boat Kateri i Radës with the Italian corvette "Sibilla", which resulted in sinking the Albanian boat resulting in more than 80 Albanian lives lost. After this tragedy, the feeling in Italy and in Europe, was that an Italian military presence in Albania would produce violent reactions. While the expected response in Albania was that there would be anger and a change of mind by Albania to cooperating with Italy, surprisingly the Albanian political leadership accepted Italy's role in the military humanitarian mission. Romano Prodi then appeared in Vlorë reassuring the support of the Italian government.

Of the 6,000 UN troops sent into Albania, more than 40 per cent were Italian. It also included 1,000 French, 700 Turks, 680 Greeks, 450 Spaniards, 400 Romanians 120 Austrians and 60 Danes (Perlmutter 1998). While there was recognition of the Italian leadership, it became clear, especially to NGOs and other refugee agencies, that Italy's role was to ensure that Albanians did not make their way to Italy. Back in Italy what was taking place was the demonising and criminalisation of Albanians in Italian society. This pervasive racism approach even touched the more liberal sections of Italy, including media outlets like La Repubblica.

With Operation Alba concluded, the Italian military presence in Albania remained under the title of the Delegation of Italian Experts (DEI), following a protocol signed between Italy and Albania in August 1997. The supposed objectives of this agreement were to assist in reorganising the Albanian Army, Navy, Air Force and Police. Between 1997 and 2005 the DEI spent Euro 8.7 million on training Albanian security personnel and a further Euro 62 million on aid.

From UN sanctions to the bombardment of Serbia

In response to the Bosnian war, from 1992 to 1995 the UN imposed an embargo on what remained of Yugoslavia. After the Srebrenica genocide in July 1995, these sanctions were lifted following the Dayton Agreement at the end of the same year. Between 1998-1999, the UN followed now by the EU and the US, imposed sanctions hoping to discourage Milošević from pursuing mass murder of the Kosovar-Albanian population. The Milošević atrocities ended up creating both mass expulsions and causing the Kosovar population to flee their territory.

It is argued that a large amount of ammunition from the Albanian revolt in 1997 ended up in the hands of Kosovar-Albanian fighters in 1998-1999. Since 1989 Ibrahim Rugova was instrumental in the organisation of structured and peaceful protests against Serbia. At the start of the breakup of Yugoslavia in 1991, Albanians became concerned about the Serbian policies in Kosovo. In 1996, the Kosovar armed resistance took on an officiality under the name of the Kosovo Liberation Army (KLA) and after Serbian crackdown and displacement of Kosovar Albanians in 1997, the KLA eventually declared war against Serbia. Although inferior in number and arms, with the help of the Albanian diaspora, the KLA provided serious opposition to Serbia. Feeling isolated, Milošević eventually accepted the demands of The Contact Group—an informal coalition of the US, Great Britain, France, Germany, Italy and Russia regarding cease-fires, immediate withdrawal of all Serbian forces from Kosovo, the return of refugees, and providing unlimited access to international peace monitors. Despite promises, none of the requests were ever implemented and it was only after the 78 days of NATO bombardment that Serbian attacks on Kosovo ended and Kosovar Albanians were allowed to return to their homes. Although Albania was coming to grips with its internal turmoil in 1997, support for Kosovar was immense hosting large numbers of Kosovar refugees and allowing Albanian territory to be used as a training base for the KLA. The Serbian Army in 1999 responded by bombing the town of Krumë in North Albania where many Kosovar refugees had sheltered.

However, despite the Albanian popular sentiment to support Kosovar, and the Albanian government decision to support sanctions against Milošević, the then Albanian President, Sali Berisha breached the embargo against ex-Yugoslavia, allowing the sale of fuel to Serbia in exchange for personal compensation. Curiously this action placed Berisha against UN and Albania's Euro-Atlantic partners – the EU and US.

Italian strategic Ostpolitik and its approach towards Albania

Throughout the 1990s and beyond, Italy's relationship with Albania was a recurring theme. Whatever the geo-political considerations which Italy may have harboured for Albania, there was no escaping that Italy was of primary importance to Albania. The proximity of the two countries to encouraging the presence of migratory patterns, direct investment, cultural links would also involve security considerations between them also. Therefore, it should come as no surprise that bilateral cooperation with Italy would be high on the Albanian agenda.

The Italian approach towards Albania especially after the end of the Hoxha era was dominated by ambiguity along with internal tensions. Initially Italy's regional policy towards the Balkans focused on Serbia as the security player. While the goal of stabilizing Serbia was important for Italy and the region, Italian actions on the ground were often focused on untenable solutions (i.e. keeping the Yugoslav Federation together), thus potentially harming Italian interests in the long run. On the other hand, Italy's initial "Albania policy" was bound in supplying economic and security aid making Italy's presence and voice an important one in Albania. However, on the whole, Italy has preferred to react rather than act on Albanian affairs largely due to the concern that Albania was a source of potential security threat rather than a potential economic partner. To some extent the tensions within the Italian "Albania policy" as well as between it and the regional policy have ultimately harmed Italian interests in the Western Balkans and have reduced its role as an agent of change.

Albanian migration to Italy

By 2010 almost half of the Albanian resident population was estimated to have emigrated and living abroad — primarily in neighbouring Greece and Italy, but also in the United Kingdom and North America. According to the official data published by the Italian government, at the end of 2020 Albanians were the second largest migrant community after that of Moroccans. However, the number of 416.703 regular Albanians reported by the Italian authorities (*Ministero del Lavoro e delle Politiche Sociali*) is based on those with valid identity documents and did not represent the entire picture. Other Albanians reside and live in Italy with short term visas but also "irregular" migrants who are working in the 'black' and waiting for the next visa waiver to obtain their permit (*permesso di soggiorno*) and thus, become "regular" migrants.

The first Albanian community to establish in Italy was in 1448 and 1459 when the King of Naples, Alfonso V and his son Ferdinand asked Skenderbeg for help. Skenderbeg initially sent a force led by Demetrio Reres to then go to Italy in person to lead the combined Napoletan-Albanian forces who were decisive to end the French-supported insurrection. After protecting Napoli, the Albanian soldiers were rewarded with land East of Taranto in Puglia from King Alfonso. From the time of Skenderbeg's death in 1468 until 1480 there were constant migration waves of Albanians to Italy. The next wave of migration was at the beginning of the sixteenth century where Albanians (called Arberesh) were encouraged by Venice to migrate from central Greece (mostly from Peloponnese) to reinforce defences of Italian Kingdoms of Naples and Venice against the Ottomans. This was a permanent move and most of descendants of Arberesh people live in South Italian regions of Puglia, Basilicata, Calabria, Sicilia, Campagnia and Molise.

While relations with Italy began to improve, in July 1990, six-thousand people forced their way into Western embassies in Tirana (Dervishi, 2006: 785). A civil truck that broke the wall-fence of the German Embassy made it easy for first Albanians to enter the Embassy premises. Unlike the Popa family incident, this was a mass response which openly challenged the regime. As others have observed unemployment, poverty and disastrous economic reasons coupled with missing political rights in Albania were the main reasons that forced these people to seek a better life (Goxha 2016: 256).

The fall of communism in 1991 did not change economic conditions in a now more divided Albanian society. Divisions amongst supporters of the old communist regime and the new Democratic Party added to economic difficulties producing empty shelves regarding very basic goods. This encouraged a mass exodus in 1991, with more than 30,000 Albanian refugees reaching Italy on rusty-old commercial boats. This caught Italian authorities unprepared and not able to offer food and accommodation to these numbers. Their legal status was unclear following the "Martelli Law", approved in February 1990. According to one view:

> The present law in fact, did not provide special protection, with the exception of persons persecuted for political reasons, because of race, religion, etc., as provided by the Geneva Convention (Goxha 2016: 259).

Initially, these "illegal" migrants were locked up in stadiums, schools and other government buildings, but under public and international pressure, the Italian government had no choice but to distribute Albanian refugees to different regions of Italy and grant them the asylum status. The EU also joined with further aid to Albania especially in 1993. Nevertheless, the Albanian migration did not stop and the response of the Italian government after the next migration wave caused by Albanian pyramid scheme collapse in 1997 was similar to that of the operation Pelican: protection of the Italian borders.

According to the Italian Statistical agency (ISTAT), at the end of 2019 some 420,000 Albanians resided in Italy (officially). This equalled over 8 per cent of all foreigners in Italy and the second largest overseas community after Romanians. This large number of Albanians registered in Italy was the clearest indication that the Italian strategy of protecting its borders from Albanian refugees had not work. At the same time the trend of Albanian migration towards Italy and other European countries in the twenty-first century has changed. If in the late twentieth century Albanians left the country due to political and economic reasons, in the twenty-first century this flight of Albanians is now due to societal breakdown, criminality and economic collapse. Moreover, the brain-drain for a small country such as Albania is damaging coupled with the fact that there is only a trickle of return migration.

In 2020 an ironic Albanian act of solidarity occurred during the

Corona virus outbreak in Northern Italy when Albania, sent 30 doctors and nurses to assist Italy's worst affected Covid19 region. At the time, Italy was one of the worst affected by the virus in terms of deaths.

The beginning of the EU era for Albania

There are two important periods in the development of relations between Albania and the EU. The first period occurred from 1990 until 1999, followed by a second phase from 2000 to this day. The first phase began with initial diplomatic relations between Albania and the European Economic Community (EEC) which occurred soon after the first Albanian multi-party elections in spring of 1991. The impetus for the diplomatic contact occurred after the student revolts in December 1990 where the Chair of the Presidium, Ramiz Alia made concessions to the protesting students. Under the slogans of "Freedom Democracy" and "We want Albania the same as Europe", Alia not wanting the same fate as Romanian Ceaușescu, accepted that these protests were a call for liberal tolerance and political pluralism. Soon after, political parties emerged including the Democratic Party as well as other political entities in Albania. The Socialist Party of Ramiz Alia won the first election and it was not until after the first free elections in the spring of 1992 that the EU signed the Trade and Cooperation Agreement with Albania.

This Agreement sought to regulate the economic and trade relations between Albania and the EEC, paving the way for closer relations. It is arguable whether this agreement offered the same outcomes to Albania as it might have to other East European countries, or that the Albanian economy was able to benefit from the PHARE program that was offered to the South-eastern European countries (Nexhipi 2019: 37). Nevertheless, this was a steppingstone in support of political developments to this fragile democracy.

Not long after the fall of the Berlin Wall, the collapse of the Soviet Union and then the disintegration of Yugoslavia saw the emergence of the Maastricht Treaty, which came into force in November 1993. Besides other major changes it also officially established the European Union in name. Almost immediately the EU began eyeing the new states from the East as new members of an enlarged European Union in an attempt to reunite the continent after the tumultuous events of the early 1990s. This new enlargement was launched by the European Council meeting of December 1997 and negotiations were conducted separately with each country. The Central and Eastern States pursued membership of the EU often in coordination with joining the security arm, NATO.

In 1995, Austria, Finland, and Sweden joined the EU and in that moment the EU had no plans for Western Balkans enlargement. The entire Balkan region was dealing with its delicate aftermath of its disintegration. The Srebrenica genocide in 1995 proved once more that ethnic hate in the Balkans was never far from the surface. Serious moves towards EU-Albanian accession discussions would have to wait another decade. Albania's own belief that its small steps on the path towards democracy allowed for it to ask the EU to begin negotiations through the Association Agreement. The European Commission on the other hand felt that insufficient progress had been made by Albania regarding democratic reforms and therefore premature to take this step at this time.

While the European Union in the early 1990s had no immediate plans to open up membership to the Western Balkans, a dialogue framework between the EU and Albania was however put in place. This allowed for legislation, custom cooperation, economic and financial, agriculture and infrastructure matters to progress. It was nonetheless delay in the late 1990s as further Albanian civil conflict negatively affected the progress and talks with the EU. Some efforts were provided to Albania and other Western Balkan countries in 1998 in order to support further economic cooperation with the European markets. This agreement included the removal of duties for goods (mainly industrial) entering the EU from Albania.

Poor economic prospects and a decline in living standards, unemployment, and poverty in the Western Balkans was again followed by a further bout of ethnic cleansing of Kosovar Albanians in 1997. The Srebrenica genocide was still fresh in the minds of Albania, and again in the eyes of Albania the EU failed again to protect Kosovar Albanians from Serbian actions. NATO diplomacy with Serbia proved unsuccessful, culminating in the 78-day bombardment that ended in June 1999. While NATO was bombarding Serbia, a new framework namely Stabilization and Association Process (SAP) was proposed to include Albania, Former Yugoslav Republic of Macedonia, Croatia, Bosnia and Herzegovina and the Federal Yugoslav Republic. The SAP paved the way for the Stabilization and Association Agreements (SAA) as a turning point for South-Eastern Europe, representing the initiation of a sustainable development process in the region. The SAA was not a simple bilateral process, but rather a Pact of Stability between Western Balkans and the European Union. This pact required all countries to cooperate with each-other, establish a common market, support internal democratization reforms as well as developing regional partnership. This initiative provided a framework for the Western Balkans to better pursue EU membership. For the first time in the bloody Balkan's history the SAA united all Western Balkan countries towards a common goal – joining the EU!

Italy was, of course, one of those countries interested in finding mechanisms to ensure long term stability in Albania. The Stability Pact for Southeast Europe, a 40-partner international initiative for the Balkan area, was signed in June 1999. While the initial focus of the Stability Pact was on conflict resolution, fighting crime and supporting economic development, migration issues were later recognised with the creation of the Migration, Asylum, and the

Refugees Return Regional Initiative.

By 1999 the Italian government had decided to formalise its own broad initiative for supporting stability in the Balkans, including Albania. In October 1999 the Italian parliament approved the Law 84 – the "Italian Participation in the Stabilisation, Reconstruction and Development of the Balkans". The law makes no reference to migratory flows, although it does concentrate on creating a steering committee to establish priority criteria for planning and providing aid in the region – criteria that later included support for managed migration flows. Surprisingly, but not really, Italian Foreign Affairs made the statement, "Albania is no longer a priority country for Italy." The extensive migratory flows have ended – because of police cooperation and the simple fact that Albania has already sent much of its labour force abroad. As profound as this statement was, Italy remained a key commercial partner for Albania exampled by the 74.8 per cent of Albanian exports it receives and provides 31.5 per cent of Albania's imports.

During the path of pursuing EU membership, Albania was informed in November 1999 that the EU Commission found that Albania had not made enough progress to be able to sign the SAA. A year later, in November 2000, Albania was again disappointed with the Zagreb Summit, which clarified that countries involved within SAA were potential EU candidates (Nexhipi 2019: 79). It was clear that Albania was not ready and in order to further Albanian progress, a High-Level Leading Group: Albania – EU was created. After a series of meeting between the EU and Albanian government in 2001 the decision to start a negotiation process, signing and monitoring the implementation of SAA was undertaken. The Council of General Issues of EU decided to start the negotiation process with Albania in October 2002. In February 2003, meetings between the Albanian delegation and the EU began in earnest.

Another crucial event that brought SAA countries of the Western

Balkans closer to EU was the Thessaloniki Summit in 2003. During the summit it was made clear that progress towards European membership would be assessed on an individual state basis based on performance regarding economic, democratic reforms, respect for human rights, good governance, and respect for the rule of law. From the evaluation report of this Summit, Albania's fate would depend on the:

> Consolidation of the good political climate and a sustainable policy for reforms [which] remains a pre-condition for further progress towards the EU. The focus should be on effective application of reforms (European Commission 2003).

In 2004, the European Commission offered a "European Partnership" proposal to Albania, a manual for candidate countries to join the EU. This Partnership Document signposted priorities of European integration in the short and medium term. It also served for Albania as a framework to measure objectives and criteria with regard to its progress towards the SAA. Albania negotiated tirelessly with the EU for a further two years, until finally, in June 2006, the Stabilization and Association Agreement was signed. A year later, in July 2007, a Central Europe Free Trade Agreement (CEFTA) was ratified and signed by all Western Balkan countries.

Albanian corruption and rule of law – The Gërdeci explosion

Albanian unreadiness to join the EU was again on display in March 2008 with destabilisation of the Gërdeci events. A major explosion of an ex-military depot shook the Albanian capital when the Albanian defence ministry had agreed to destroy old stockpiles of ageing Chinese ammunitions at the ex-military base of Gërdeci, some 14 kilometres from Tirana. An American company, the Southern Ammunition Company Inc. (SAC), was licenced in 2006 by the Albanian Defence Ministry to destroy millions of bullets remnant from the communist period. SAC subcontracted an Albanian company, Alb-Demil, which would undertake the task. The reckless approach in destroying the armaments resulted in 26 deaths and over 300 injured people, 2,306 surrounding buildings were damaged or destroyed (Usatoday.com, 2008). The blame for this event rested on the shoulders of the Albanian Defence Minister, Fatmir Mediu, who resigned soon after the explosions but not surprisingly avoided prosecution. Months later Kosta Trebicka, a whistle-blower in the government, who had directly accused the son of Prime Minister Berisha of corrupt practices died in mysterious circumstances. Trebicka was contracted and involved in repackaging the Albanian ammunition that was being sold to AEY Inc, another U.S. firm that was contracted by the Pentagon to supply the Afghan army (Koleka, 2008). In 2022 families are still waiting for justice for the victims, the Albanian justice system showed once more its failure to provide justice and equality before the law – one of the reasons the EU extended its mandatory-long list of conditions to prepare Albania for membership.

Of the EU Commission recommended 12 key priorities to Albania in 2010, the first one states: "Ensuring a good functioning for the Parliament based on a constructive and sustainable political dialogue among all political parties" (European Commission, 2010: 11). It was exactly the malfunctioning of the Parliament and non-existent political dialogue that fuelled the political instability in January 2011.

Unable to win a majority in the Albanian 2009 parliamentary elections, the PD was forced to forge a coalition with the Levizja Socialiste per Integrim [Socialist movement for integration] (LSI). More evidence emerged of political corruption within the government were revealed only plunging the country into further political chaos (Likmeta, 2011). The opposition demanded the resignation of Prime Minister Berisha, calling new elections. Together with the Gërdeci explosion in 2008 and the death of innocent people on 21 January 2011, evidenced the ubiquitous political corruption and dysfunctional parliament.

More waiting and more conditions...on Albanian EU membership

The Albanian government took a very ambitious approach on a 5-year National Plan for Applying the SAA 2007-2012, which was "benefiting the status of a candidate country for EU membership within a two-year period" (*Keshilli i Ministrave*, 2008:15). A month after the SAA was ratified, in April 2009, Albania submitted a full application for EU membership. In order to comply with Thessaloniki Summit commitment on visa liberalization for the Western Balkans, visa liberalization was granted for Albanian citizens at the end of 2010.

As a result of a contested parliamentary elections won by the PD in 2009, some 200 Socialist Party members went on a hunger strike in 2010, which lasted for 19 days. It was another reason for the European Commission to point out that:

> the political cramp is damaging the democracy in Albania and is preventing important reforms which are necessary for the country's progress towards the EU integration and rule of law function (European Commission, 2010: 12).

That was enough for the European Commission to place the following 12 recommendations on Albania:

1. Ensuring a good functioning for the Parliament based on a constructive and sustainable political dialogue among all political parties.

2. Approving pending laws which require a Parliament majority.

3. Appointing the Ombudsman and ensuring a regular hearing and voting process in Parliament for appointing at the Constitutional and Supreme Courts.

4. Modification of the legal framework for elections, in accordance to OSCE-ODIHR recommendations.

5. Holding elections based on European and international standards.

6. Essential full steps in public administration reform.

7. Fostering rule of law through approving and applying a reforming strategy for the justice system, ensuring independence, efficiency and accountability of justice institutions.

8. Effective application of the strategy and the Government's action plan against corruption on all levels.

9. Intensification of the fight against organized crime.

10. Preparation, approval and application of a national strategy and action plan on the property rights.

11. Undertaking of concrete steps in protecting the human rights, especially women, children and Roma people and applying anti-discrimination policies effectively.

12. Undertaking additional measures for improving the treatment of detained persons in police stations, custody and penitentiary institutions (European Commission, 2010: 11-12).

The EU Commission assessed the progress made by Albania in 2012 and in usual EU double speak it found that "Albania had made some progress in meeting the political criteria for EU membership, with its series of reforms based on the 12 key priorities" (European Commission, 2012: 14). On closer examination, the Commission however found that sufficient progress was only made on 4 of 12 key points, it nonetheless recommended to the EU Council that it approve Albania with the candidate country status. The Council pre-conditioned the progress on the Albanian Parliamentary elections in 2013, which were considered by the EU as being positive. This was a step forward for the Council to finally approve Albania's candidate status. However, the council added another 5 conditions for progress with Albania's membership be pursued before the start of the negotiations on EU membership. These included:

1. Application of public administration reform in order to increase the

professionalism and depoliticization of the public administration;

2. Further actions in fostering independence, efficiency and accountability of judicial institutions;

3. Further efforts against corruption, aiming to establish a permanent registry of proactive investigations, prosecutions and punishment;

4. Further efforts in the fight against organized crime, including the establishment of a permanent registry of proactive investigations, prosecutions and punishment;

5. Effective measures in protecting the human rights, including Roma people, anti-discriminating measures and property rights to be applied (European Commission, 2013: 18-19).

Only in July 2014 the EU Council decided that Albania become an EU candidate country, and noted with "appreciation for applied reforms, and encouragement as well for increasing the flow of reforms" (European Commission, 2014: 1). Since then, Albania has not made significant progress in pursuance of membership given the major concerns over "political instability, political polarization, fragile democracy; lack of democratic culture; corruption and organized crime [that] are obstacles for Albania's EU integration process" (Nexhipi, 2019: 47) which continue to inflict it.

Albania's security dilemma at rest – NATO membership

After a long and drawn-out negotiation, in 2009 Albania was eventually admitted into the North Atlantic Treaty Organisation (NATO). This process began in early 1992 when Albania joined the newly created North Atlantic Cooperation Council, renamed the Euro-Atlantic Partnership Council in 1997. Since then, the Albanian armed forces have participated in peaceful missions in Bosnia and Herzegovina in 1996, as well as combat missions such in Afghanistan. NATO established a logistical base in Tirana which became operable for its bombardment in 1999, and in 2002, the NATO HQ Tirana was established to support Albanian defence capability reforms as well as to contribute to the command and control of KFOR. This has allowed NATO to undertake closer collaboration with Albanian security forces and increase Albanian defence capabilities. The result was "Defender 21", which in 2021 used the Albanian land, naval and air space in a way never seen before in the Western Balkans. NATO recently accepted the proposal of the Albanian government to build a permanent military base in its territory. This news was welcomed by many Albanians and was also seen as a buttress against its neighbourhood foes Greece, Serbia, and to a lesser extent, Italy.

6

The European Union and the accession of the Western Balkans

Enlargement towards the Western Balkans has been described in several ways: the inevitable conclusion of the enlargements to the countries formerly behind the Iron Curtain, the democratic anchor of politically unstable countries, or the inclusion of the only European countries not yet members of the EU. Some have even defined the Western Balkans as the "Achille's heel" of Europe (Bogdani and Loughlin, 2007: 87). What is certain is that in all EU maps, the Western Balkans appear like an "unnatural grey zone". The prevalent approach to the Western Balkans enlargement has emphasized the role of the EU institution, with the Western Balkans relegated to the role of states looking for EU membership. Hence, the literature describing the process of enlargement, the Europeanization of the Western Balkans, the policy instruments adopted by the EU and the Western Balkans' inefficiency to reach the necessary standard to become EU members is abundant.

However, the story is more complicated for at least three reasons. The first one refers to the fact that the Western Balkans are not a uniform group of countries. Quite the contrary, they have different political, social and economic dynamics, they feature with different levels of democratization and they have different national interests. Secondly, the EU Member States have different points of view about the EU enlargement towards the Western Balkans. Moreover, they also have different capacities with which they can steer the negotiation process.

Thirdly, the enlargement towards the Western Balkans is conditioned by political dynamics transcending the Western Balkans per se. For example, the UK's exit from the EU has somehow slowed down the enlargement process because, for a long time, the UK has been one of the Member States more in favour of the inclusion of the Western Balkans in the EU. The position of the UK was not directly linked to the British interests in the region and the inclusion of new countries into the EU was for the UK another way to stop any attempt to make the EU more federal.

As a consequence, the story of EU policy toward the Western Balkans is not just the story of how the EU institutions promoted enlargement and the decisions adopted. It is the story about the different perspectives and expectations that the Western Balkans have on EU enlargement as well as the story about the different national policies of the EU Member States toward the Western Balkans. Moreover, these two perspectives are fundamentally interlinked. The resulting picture is much more multi-faceted, but also more useful in interpreting the stalemate characterizing the EU uncertainties (if not ambiguities) toward this new enlargement.

This chapter aims to examine the broad policy questions involved in the problematic relationship between the EU and the Western Balkans, with a particular emphasis on Albania. Firstly, there is a review of the reasons – most of which are fairly well known – of the so-called EU enlargement fatigue. Secondly, the chapter discusses the Euro-sceptical views of the Western Balkans, which are much less known in contrast to the EU enlargement fatigue. Thirdly, there is a tentative exploration of the viewpoints of the EU member states toward the enlargement of the Western Balkans.

The Goal of Membership

The inclusion of the Western Balkan states in the EU is widely considered as the only feasible political, economic and social prospect for the countries in the region. Since the end of the 1990s-early 2000s, the EU has espoused an open-door policy towards the Balkans. The results of the 1999 European Council meeting in Cologne was resolute. In its conclusions, pages were dedicated to the Western Balkans and South-Eastern Europe. Even if, at that time, the Western Balkans were considered a question of "External relations" and not "Enlargement", the European Council adopted an ambitious Stability Pact for South-Eastern Europe that "will help to enhance peace, stability and prosperity in, and cooperation between, countries in the region". It declared:

> The European Council reaffirms the readiness of the European Union to draw the countries of this region closer to the prospect of full integration into its structures. This will be done through a new kind of contractual relationship taking into account the individual situations of each country, including progress in regional cooperation, and with a prospect of European Union membership based on the Amsterdam Treaty and fulfilment of the criteria defined at the Copenhagen European Council in June 1993 (Council of the European Union, 1999, points 71 & 72).

The EU enlargement policy has taken its present form by being reshaped with each new enlargement wave. In particular, the 2004-2007 enlargements of Central and Eastern European countries shaped its current approach, strictly based on the respect of the "conditionality" principle. Accession conditionality can be briefly defined as the sum of the obligations that the countries applying to become EU members have to undertake before their accession.

The "Copenhagen Criteria" defined at the Copenhagen European Summit in 1993, established the guiding principles for the countries wishing to become members of the EU. Only when the candidate countries fulfil those requirements will the EU start the negotiations. Subsequently, at the Madrid Summit held on 15-16 December 1995, the EU through the so-called "Madrid Criteria" mandated that the candidate states are not only responsible for transposing the EU acquis Communautaire into their internal legal framework, but are also responsible for establishing the administrative and legal structures in charge of implementing the legislation they are harmonizing.

In addition to these criteria, Agenda 2000 also identifies the establishment of good neighbourly relations as a condition of accession which expects all candidate countries should resolve border disputes between themselves and with third countries before joining the Union and, if necessary, apply to the International Court of Justice for its resolution. Last, but not least, the European Commission also introduced "technical criteria" for the opening and closing of the negotiation headings known as "chapters", each of which represents the different policy areas of the EU. Considering the turbulent political domestic conditions of the Western Balkans states, the European Commission particularly emphasized the importance of Chapter 23 on Judiciary and Fundamental Rights and the Chapter 24 on Justice, Freedom and Security, agreeing that these chapters should be addressed as early as possible and remain open throughout the negotiation process and that they will eventually affect the judgment over all other chapters.

Despite all these requirements, the EU always showed a favourable approach towards the Western Balkans. For example, in 2000, at Santa Maria de Feira, the European Council affirmed that the Western Balkan countries were "potential candidates for EU membership" even before the signature of an Association Agreement, the formal first step toward any enlargement (Council of the European Union, 19-20 June 2000: point 67). Three years later, in 2003, the Thessaloniki European Council went further by declaring that "the future of the Balkans is in the European Union," (Council of the European Union,

19-20 June 2003: point 40) and that accession to the EU would be dependent upon fulfilling the same requirements applied to Central and Eastern European (CEE) states. The Association and Stabilization Process (SAP) became the official EU enlargement policy towards the region (Pippan, 2004). The promise of association and eventual membership changed the relationship between the Western Balkans and the EU since it provided the region with a set of yardsticks to use and measure their advance towards Europe, and the Union with the opportunity to deploy the full strength of political conditionality (Van Meurs 2003).

Moreover, the International Commission on the Balkans, chaired by Giuliano Amato, declared that:

> There is an urgent need to solve the outstanding status and constitutional issues in the Balkans and to move the region as a whole from the stage of protectorates and weak states to the stage of EU accession. This is the only way to prevent the Western Balkans from turning into the black hole of Europe. (…) The question today is no longer, 'What should be done?' We should clearly bring the region into the EU. Rather we need to establish the sequence of policy steps to be undertaken and the structure of the incentives that will make them work. We need policies so that the region can get on, get in and catch up with the rest of Europe (Amato, 2005).

More recently, in February 2020 the European Commission presented a Communication on "Enhancing the accession process - A credible EU perspective for the Western Balkans" (European Commission 2020). From the communication, one can read that:

> The European Union and its Member States have consistently, since the Feira and Thessaloniki Summits in 2000 and 2003, expressed their unequivocal support for the European perspective of the Western Balkans. The Council conclusions adopted at the General Affairs Council in June 2019 has also

reaffirmed 'its commitment to enlargement, which remains a key policy of the European Union, in line with the renewed consensus on enlargement approved by the European Council on 14 and 15 December 2006 and subsequent Council conclusions' (European Commission 2020).

In the same communication, the full membership of the Western Balkans is defined as a political, security and economic interest of the EU. For this reason, and to make the accession process more credible and predictable, the Commission proposed some methodological changes in the enlargement policy, particularly for the accession process for North Macedonia and Albania, but, upon agreement, Serbia and Montenegro could also be part of this new method. The Commission's proposals were adopted by the member states on 25 March 2020 EU General Affairs Council. In addition, on 15 May 2020, Montenegro announced that they accepted to be part of the new method proposed.

The integration prospect, together with the related implementation programs, meant a significant improvement vis-à-vis previous international policies towards the region (Belloni, 2009). At last, after years of competing strategies with contradictory impact on the ground, EU member states agreed that the Western Balkans should belong to Europe and, thus, gave the region both a vision for its future and a concrete goal to achieve. In offering an integration perspective, EU member states hoped that Europe's attractiveness would provide a positive reforming influence on local political elites without the imposition of Western institutions and policies. The application of political conditionality was expected to support progress in meeting the requirements for EU membership. In particular, the EU hoped to strengthen supporters of reform, while at the same time weakening opposition to, and thus tipping the balance in favour of change (European Stability Initiative, 2005).

As it turned out, the EU's approach towards the Western Balkans has led to significant changes, but considerable debate remains on whether the glass is half full or half empty. Setting aside Slovenia, whose European future was never seriously questioned and joined the EU as early as 2004, the other states proceeded towards EU membership at a different speed and with different results. Croatia officially joined the EU on 1 July 2013, while the other Western Balkan states made some progress towards that goal. Albania, Macedonia, Montenegro and Serbia have obtained EU candidate status, with all of them having started membership negotiations.

Table 6.1. The EU enlargement to the Western Balkans: an overview

	Association agreement (signed)	Membership application	Commission opinion	Accession negotiations (start / end)	Accession
Slovenia	June 1996	June 1996	July 1997	Mar. 1998-Dec. 2002	May 2004
Croatia	Oct. 2001	Feb. 2003	Apr. 2004	Oct. 2005-Dec. 2011	Jul. 2013
Montenegro	Oct. 2007	Dec. 2008	Nov. 2010	June 2012	
Serbia	May 2008	Dec. 2009	Oct. 2011	Jan. 2014	
North Macedonia	Apr. 2001	Mar. 2004	Nov. 2005*	July 2022	
Albania	June 2006	Apr. 2009	Nov. 2010**	July 2022	
Bosnia-Herzegovina	June 2008	Feb. 2016	May 2019		
Kosovo***	Initialed Aug. 2014				

Notes: * Commission has recommended opening accession negotiations since 2009, but Greece and Bulgaria have blocked it until July 2022.

** The European Council granted "candidate status" in June 2014; blocked by Greece and then granted together with North Macedonia in July 2022.

*** Independence non recognized by Cyprus, Greece, Romania, Slovakia, and Spain.

Source: Sedelmeier 2015, updated by the Authors.

Bosnia-Herzegovina and Kosovo – both currently recognized as potential candidates for EU membership – constitute the most problematic cases. Bosnia's internal political and economic struggles have been hindering its path towards closer links with European institutions while popular malcontent over corruption, poor governance and unemployment flaring up in early 2014 has raised alarm bells even among EU bureaucrats (Belloni, Ramovic, & Kappler, 2016). In an attempt to reboot EU-Bosnia relations, the EU approved the Stabilisation and Association Agreement's entry into force on 16 March 2015, in exchange for a pledge by Bosnian authorities to adopt the reforms requested for European integration at a later stage. In February 2016 Bosnia applied for EU membership but, despite the approval of the Commission's opinion in May 2019, it has not yet obtained the green light from the European Council. As for Kosovo, its independence is not recognized by Serbia or by five EU member states (Spain, Slovakia, Romania, Greece and Cyprus). This situation creates enormous obstacles for its progress towards the EU, despite the fact that Kosovo, like all other Western Balkan states, is anchored to the framework of the Stabilization and Association Process (Economides & Ker-Lindsay, 2015). Overall, the difficulties in the path to accession are perhaps best reflected in the still limited democratic character that the Western Balkan states have reached since they gained independence. According to Freedom House, there is no consolidated democratic regime in the region (Freedom House 2014). Only Croatia, which joined the EU in July 2013, is considered a "semi-consolidated" democracy in light of its extensive levels of corruption, the presence of an overwhelmed court system and its limitations on media freedom.

Nor was the case of Albania smooth either. As will be discussed more in detail, Albania declared its interest in joining the EU in April 2009, despite the cold approach of the Commission, according to which "the time was not yet ripe" (Sedelmeier, 2015: 414). Quite surprisingly, a group of EU Member States led by Germany and The Netherlands, subsequently blocked the Council's request to work on the Commission's opinion on this application (and, also on the application of Montenegro) delaying the further steps until June 2014.

Despite these specific stories, all Western Balkan states have developed various links with the EU, progressed in their contractual relation with it – above all by signing Stabilization and Association Agreements - and, in the process, settled some of their outstanding disputes. For example, the 2009 border demarcation agreement between Macedonia and Kosovo and, above all, the 2013 Serbia-Kosovo agreement which granted extensive local autonomy to Serbian municipalities in Northern Kosovo while formally integrating these municipalities into the Kosovar state, would have been impossible without significant EU involvement. At the same time, however, Western Balkan states have been less satisfactory in the speed and depth of their political, economic and social transformation than what EU leaders expected when, in 2000, they began opening their doors to the Southeast European region. Since the outbreak of the global financial and economic crisis in 2008, and particularly after the June 2016 vote in the UK in favour of leaving the EU, the "pull of Brussels" has progressively weakened.

Turning the Integration Goal into a Mirage?

Without doubt, the global economic and financial crisis in 2008 also affected the enlargement perspectives of the Western Balkans. More in general, the crisis revealed the citizen's idea about a real or perceived slowness of the integration process. However, a certain "enlargement fatigue" was present even before and, quite paradoxically, coincided with the success of 2004-2007 enlargements to 12 new member states in Central and Eastern Europe. In an article which appeared in *The Financial Times* in 2002, Martin Wolf argued that:

> The EU is caught between the lure of the desirable and fear of the unworkable. (…) Yet further enlargement now seems

inescapable. It offers big benefits and equally huge challenges. Making it work will exhaust the energies of Europe for decades to come (Wolf 2002).

This approach was reaffirmed by the Commissioner for External Relations, Chris Patten ahead of the Thessaloniki Summit of June 2003, by saying:

> Thessaloniki [Summit] will send two important messages to the Western Balkans: The prospect of membership of the EU is real, and we will not regard the map of the Union as complete until you have joined us. We in the European Commission will do all we can to help you succeed. But membership must be earned. It will take the sheer hard work and applied political will of those in power in the region. How far you proceed along the road towards European Integration, and how fast, will be up to you (European Commission 2003).

It is plausible that also the unexpected results of the 2005 French and Dutch referenda on the Constitutional Treaty reinforced the idea that enlargements were to be seriously reconsidered. Another alarm bell was the results of the Eurobarometer 63 released by the European Commission in July 2005. According to this research, only half of the respondents in the then 25 member states were in favour of further enlargements of the EU. While the Support for further enlargement was stronger in the ten new member states, the size of the difference between the results obtained in the fifteen old member states and the ten new member states (27 points) highlighted the diversity of opinion with regard to the geographical evolution of the European Union, with 60% of respondents in Germany and Luxembourg, 58% in Austria and in France declaring reluctance, if not opposition to further enlargement. Moreover, clear majority of citizens were opposed to membership being granted to Turkey or Albania: 52% and 50% respectively of citizens were opposed to their accession (European Commission 2005). Thus, it was not surprising if some of the EU political elite denounced the "psychological problem" for Western Europe and now enlarging the club into the Balkans (Bogdani & Loughlin, 2007).

One should also not underestimate the rise of Islamophobia within the internal politics of some Member States (Jackson 2018). By way of example, more than 60 per cent of the Albanian population is Muslim, and 25 per cent of the population of North Macedonia are ethnic Albanians who share the Muslim faith. As Hoxhaj (2021: 153) has emphasised, "there are [EU] Member States uncomfortable with the idea of a country with a large Muslim majority ever joining the EU". However, at the moment, the EU does not express this openly as a determining factor, and the main debate about the EU enlargement towards the Western Balkans is focused on issues such as the level of corruption, organised crime and state capture, as well as the respect of the rule of law.

As mentioned, the 2008 economic and financial crisis also played a role in the "Enlargement fatigue". Within EU member states, the crisis enlarged the chasm between institutions and citizens. Many European citizens considered (and still consider) their institutions as arcane and distant bodies unable to provide concrete answers to their real or perceived problems and, in some cases, even responsible for their increasing difficulties. Unsurprisingly, the 2015 Eurobarometer has recorded little backing for the EU: 57% of all EU citizens have either a neutral or negative image of the Union while one every two citizens believe their voice and input is meaningless (that is, "does not count") within the EU decision-making process (Eurobarometer 2015). Given this mistrust, national political elites within EU member states have frequently used the EU as a scapegoat for their own failures – thus augmenting a negative perception and critical assessment of European institutions. In this climate, both right-wing and left-wing political parties and groups, with the former more vociferous than the latter, have loudly condemned the European integration process as technocratic, undemocratic, expensive, intrusive and ultimately damaging to European citizens.

In a context marked by a profound economic and financial crisis and significant anti-EU attitudes, the prospects of enlargement to the Western Balkans have taken a back seat. As Dimitar Bechev has argued, the Euro crisis may not have killed the EU enlargement policy, but it has relegated the Western Balkans to "the outermost circle in a multi-speed Europe – the periphery of the periphery" (Bechev 2012: 1) - while strengthening a "wait-and-see" attitude towards the region (Grabbe, Knaus & Korski, 2010). While Germany remained a staunch supporter of EU enlargement, conditional upon the fulfilment of strict criteria by aspiring EU members, many EU member states believe that they should focus their energies on sorting out their own internal economic and financial difficulties before seriously considering how (and whether) to proceed with accepting new members. This diffuse indifference combined with European citizens' scepticism in turning enlargement into anything but a priority (Balfour & Stratulat, 2015). Since 2008 support for EU enlargement has decreased dramatically in Cyprus, the Czech Republic, Italy, Spain, Slovakia and Slovenia, opposition to enlargement has increased by more than 20 percent in 5 years. Overall, popular opposition to enlargement is 49 percent throughout the 28 EU member states (Eurobarometer 2015). Some differences still exist with regard to this hostility vis-à-vis new aspiring members, with most opposition being expressed towards Albania and Kosovo (Eurobarometer 2011).

Not only have EU member states and their citizens shown limited enthusiasm about accepting new member states from the Western Balkans, but equally the European Commission has lowered its level of activism in favour of and commitment to enlargement – at least compared to the important, supportive and instrumental role it previously played in the process of accession of CEE states. The EU commitment to the region has been more ambiguous than it is often asserted in academic analysis, eschewing both explicit indications of accession and even references to membership timetables. Indeed, as

David Phinnemore has argued, the European Council has promoted the region's "European perspective," but has not spoken of "either destiny or that the Western Balkan countries 'shall' become members," raising questions about the idea of a supposed inevitability of accession to the Union or, as Phinnemore put it, "about when – indeed if – all the Western Balkan countries will actually achieve their goal of EU membership" (Phinnemore 2013: 29, 34).

This attitude is both a reflection of member states' preferences and of the need to strengthen EU structures after the Union quickly grew to 28 members (27 after Brexit). Since 2006 the Commission has linked future EU expansion to no less than the comprehensive reform of the EU's institutions, policies and budget (European Commission 2006) – a still widely held view among policymakers in Brussels despite the coming into force of the Lisbon treaty on 1 December 2009. Not only has the Union's "integration capacity" been greatly tested by several rounds of enlargement, leading to a sort of "Balkanization of the EU" rather than a "Europeanization of the Balkans," but also difficulties experienced with some of the latest arrivals to the EU club – such as Bulgaria and Romania. These two states joined the Union in 2007 and have contributed to raising the bar for current and potential candidates (O'Brennan, 2014). As a result, while the EU has made accession conditional on the fulfilment of criteria first outlined at the 1993 Copenhagen Council (which were initially conceived of as a framework for aspiring new members from the CEE, and included the existence of stable democratic institutions, a functioning market economy and the ability to adopt the *acquis communautaire*), it has drawn lessons from past enlargement mistakes and turned these criteria into an obstacle for aspiring new members, rather than a guide to carrying out domestic reforms needed to obtain membership.

Since 1993 the *acquis communautaire* has grown to about 140,000 pages long – inevitably increasing the political and bureaucratic difficulty to transpose and implement this expanding body of EU legislation to aspiring new members. In addition, not only has the acquis grown, but also the Copenhagen criteria have expanded considerably. While becoming more detailed, they have paradoxically been subjected to increasing differences in interpretation, thus failing to be a reliable tool to measure candidate countries' progress by (Kochenov 2004). In addition, because of the disappointing situation of both Bulgaria and Romania – both plagued by serious governance problems - the negotiation with candidate states currently starts with the chapters on judiciary, justice and home affairs, which are generally the most difficult topics to address. Most importantly, besides the Copenhagen criteria member states within the European Council have put forward different conditions for each candidate state, inevitably raising questions about the fairness and credibility of the accession process and prompting candidate states to complain about "double standards" and "moving targets" being applied to them (European Stability Initiative, 2014: 5).

The difficulty to comply with European demands has been augmented on the ground, where European institutions have been frequently unable to project a coherent vision and strategy. In Kosovo, for example, EU activities have been scattered across six different institutions, with significant problems of coherence and coordination (Papadimitriou & Petrov, 2013: 123). In Bosnia, a turf war among EU member states (above all between Germany and the UK) has weakened the effectiveness of European actors who, faced by domestic resistance to change, eventually refrained from applying conditionality and even abandoned or ignored previously stated reform priorities, criteria and conditions (Bassuener & Weber, 2013). In Montenegro, local NGOs have discredited EU staff by criticizing accession reports for being too soft with the Montenegro government. Likewise, in North Macedonia EU bureaucrats are reproached for ultimately focusing more on self-adulation with regard to their contribution to the development of a "success story" in the Western Balkans, rather than providing a genuine assessment of the situation in the country (European Stability Initiative, 2014: 15-17).

In this context of uncertain and wavering commitment by both EU institutions and member states, compounded by significant implementation problems, '[t]he UK's departure from the EU may be the last nail in the coffin for accession' (Bieber 2000). As Florian Bieber argues, as a result of the so-called Brexit, the EU's ability to exert a positive influence on the region has further decreased. First, the UK's departure from the EU means the loss of one of the few remaining advocates of enlargement. Second, the EU's existential crisis is likely to strengthen the perspectives of those in the Western Balkans who question the wisdom of implementing painful reforms in order to accede to an institution whose survival in the current form is increasingly called into question by its own current members (Bieber 2000). In light of this situation, it is unsurprising that some leaders in the Western Balkans have reacted to "Brexit" by challenging the EU's celebrated transformative power (Kostovicova, 2016).

The stubborn persistence of bilateral issues among states in the region contributes to further complicate the integration process. These disputes have deep roots, frequently predating even the break-up of Yugoslavia, and including a number of problematic issues such as border demarcation, property rights, the recognition of minority rights, the rights of refugees and displaced persons, and hard-to-reconcile interpretations of history (Fouéré 2014). The most intractable of these issues was the name controversy dividing the Republic of Macedonia and Greece, with the latter objecting to the use of the name "Macedonia" by its neighbour because of historical and territorial concerns. The relationship between Croatia and Serbia also remains problematic. Tensions between the two countries have persisted, in various forms, since the process of Yugoslav dissolution began in the early 1990s (Milekic & Pantovic, 2016). For example, both countries have filed a genocide suit against each other. Although Serbia on multiple occasions has proposed the mutual withdrawal of lawsuits in favour of extra-judicial means to solve the problems inherited from the conflicts in the 1990s, (B92.net, 2014) the initial case progressed through the preliminary steps and opened at the International Court of Justice at The Hague in early 2014. In early 2015 the Court rejected the case, but Croatia's uncompromising stance raised doubts about its declared goodwill to support Serbia (and the other Western Balkan membership hopefuls) in its road towards EU integration.

In sum, the economic and financial crisis beginning in 2008 has severely weakened the EU enlargement enthusiasm. The Covid-19 pandemic which started in 2020 further reinforced this tendency. While it is undeniable that enlargement policy has not been discarded per se, it is also excessive to argue that, as a result of the geopolitical benefits enlargement brings to EU member states, "the underlying dynamics of enlargement remain largely the same" (Vachudova 2014). Rather, with various degrees of regional stability in place, and with strategic attention focused on areas like the Middle East, North Africa, and those states buffered between the EU and Russia, the geopolitical benefits of enlargement are both decreasing and changing. Rather than being primarily concerned with stability and democratic consolidation – issues that have driven Europe's approach to the region over the last 15 years – it is Russia's offensive in Ukraine in 2014 and 2021 which has revived some European interest towards the Western Balkans. Serbia's increasingly strong political and economic ties with Russia, as well as with China, represent an alarm bell for European policymakers about the dangers that a stalemate in the accession process might bring about. While Russian and Chinese diplomatic and economic advances in the region may eventually lead to the adoption of a more proactive policy, for the time being both EU member states and the European Commission have postponed any new membership in the future, without any certainty about the length of the integration process or, even, its outcome. The EU is suffering more than just "enlargement fatigue," which would suggest merely a temporary hiccup in the enlargement process; rather, the current situation is better described as a "chronic ailment" (European Stability Initiative, 2014).

The Outside-In Perspective

The prevailing approach on European enlargement takes as its point of departure the perspective, interests and strategies of European institutions and EU member states. For example, the so-called "integration capacity" focuses on the EU's ability of accepting new member states without jeopardizing its decision-making processes and operational procedures, with little or no reference to the perspectives, interests and strategies of Western Balkan states and their citizens. It is simply taken for granted that they have no choice other than to accept that integration into Euro-Atlantic institutions is the "only game in town." However, this approach is not justified because it underestimates the relevance of the point of view of the Western Balkans and the fact that the EU enlargement is a question of domestic and foreign policy in those countries.

Since 2008 the resistance to the EU membership in the Western Balkans has been growing. The EU is less attractive today than it was in 2003 when it promised an open-door policy. Indeed, Europe's current attractiveness is easily overstated. According to Börzel, "whether the 'golden carrot' [of EU accession] is big enough to draw the Western Balkans closer to Europe is still an open question" (Börzel, 2013: 175). The attitude prevailing in the Western Balkans is a mix of resignation, fatalistic Euro-realism and growing Euro-scepticism. Most citizens still see further integration into the EU as inevitable, although support for the process has declined everywhere, in some places considerably (Belloni, 2014). In extreme cases such as North Macedonia, civil society activists even argue that the country's ultimate goal is no longer that of joining the EU (and NATO), but that of establishing closer diplomatic links with Serbia (Rizinski 2014). In general, where the process of European integration is more advanced, the more pronounced the Euroscepticism. In Croatia, the youngest EU member state, support for EU integration was around 85% when the country applied for membership in 2003. In 2012, 66.2% of citizens voted "yes" in the referendum on admission to the Union, but only 43.5% of all citizens actually went to the polls. In Serbia, which started accession negotiations in January 2014, only 36% of citizens believe that joining the EU would be a "good thing" – among the lower support for European integration recorded in a candidate country (Eurobarometer 2015). In comparison, 90 per cent of Albanians are in favour of joining the EU.

Research on EU accession by CEE states has found a similar process of growing disillusionment and Euroscepticism in the candidates' progression towards membership (Taggart & Szczerbiak 2001). As the citizens learn more about the social costs of accession, they begin to wonder whether the costs outweigh the benefits, while political elites are tempted to shift the blame for painful and unpopular policy decisions to European bureaucrats and EU demands. While this mechanism is at play also in the Western Balkans, it is not only the progress in the accession process that generates negative reactions. In addition to the long-term, likely negative impact of Brexit on the EU's attractiveness, there are at least four additional underlying reasons that contribute to a growing Euroscepticism.

First, the economic, political and social difficulties experienced by neighbouring EU member states constitute a warning for aspiring new EU members. To begin with, the ruinous impact of the Euro-crisis on Greece has both negatively influenced the Western Balkans in the areas of trade, banking and remittances, (O'Brennan, 2014) and deepened scepticism among aspiring new EU members. Until a few years ago, Western Balkan states considered Greece as a successful example of a country that made visible improvements from a condition of relative backwardness and underdevelopment to stability and prosperity as a member of the Union. In addition, Greece acted as a vocal advocate on behalf of Western Balkan accession – a role that increased its popularity in the region. Greece's predicament over the last few years raises serious doubts about the supposed advantages that the process of European integration is expected to bring about (Panagiotou, 2013). The EU integration model of convergence – whereby economic laggards, by virtue of membership in the EU, would catch up with the most performing economies – has suffered a serious blow as a result of the dramatic Greek economic, political and social crisis. Greece teaches aspiring new members that the economic returns deriving from EU-directed structural reforms cannot be taken for granted. The worsening economic and political situation in other neighbouring states, above all in Bulgaria and Slovenia during 2012-2013, similarly lessens considerably any Euro-enthusiasm (O' Brennan, 2013).

Second, political and cultural elites in the Western Balkans resent what they consider to be a paternalistic attitude by European institutions. While in theory the integration process involves, on the one hand, European bureaucrats and policymakers and, on the other hand, democratically elected representatives of aspiring new members, both on a formally equal status, in practice decisions about where, how and above all when enlargement will take place are taken (or, it could be said, imposed) by Brussels. Concepts such as "democratic governance" and "rule of law" are subjected to multiple, and perhaps arbitrary, understandings providing ample opportunities to European policymakers to apply discretion in their decision. More generally, Brussels' demands that aspiring new members comply with values and principles which are seriously challenged within the Union itself by the growth of far-right Eurosceptic parties and by the return to nationalist policies are perplexing. Perhaps unsurprisingly, political elites in the Western Balkans, not unlike other elites within EU member states, are suspicious of Brussels' demands – considered as unrealistic, rigid and, to the extent they clash with citizens' expectations, undemocratic.

Third, in addition to scepticism towards the EU due to the Union's policy demands, there exist within the Western Balkans a deep-rooted mistrust and suspicion towards the Christian-Catholic Western Europe. While the Muslim population in the region, especially in Bosnia, displays various degrees of Europhilia, the same cannot be said of the Christian-Orthodox people whose hostility towards the "West" has deep historical roots. Since the late Byzantine period onwards, the Christian-Orthodox community has considered the "West" (and, later, "Europe") as the main source of danger for them, coming to prefer Ottoman rule to subordination to Rome and the Vatican (Makrides, 2009). More recently, European policy towards the region has strengthened a perception of mistrust among nationalists of the Orthodox religion – in particular Serb nationalists. Indeed, European members of NATO actively participated in the 1999 bombing of Serbia, and later requested Serbia to fully cooperate with the International Criminal Tribunal for the Former Yugoslavia – an institution which tried and condemned several Serbs involved in the war of Yugoslav dissolution in the 1990s. For many Serbs, thus, the most dangerous threat to their survival and identity comes from Europe.

Finally, while integration into the EU carries some obvious economic advantages (such as, for example, access to bailout funds), various forms of economic integration between the EU and the Western Balkans already exist (Bartlett & Prica, 2013), making the lure of full membership less attractive. Trade liberalization between the EU and the region has been achieved and has effectively eliminated all restrictions on the entry of Western Balkan products into the EU. Almost two-thirds of all commercial exchange takes place between the region and the Union. Both Montenegro and Kosovo have unilaterally adopted the euro as their currency, while Bosnia's currency, the convertible mark, is pegged to the euro. A 2006 Treaty has created an internal market in electricity and natural gas between EU member states and seven states from the region. Since December 2009 citizens of Macedonia, Montenegro and Serbia enjoy visa-free access to the Schengen area - a privilege granted in late 2010 to both Albanians and Bosnians as well. In the area of research cooperation western Balkan states (plus Turkey, minus Kosovo) have obtained a status of associated countries within the Framework Programme Seven, whereby they have become eligible for funding on the same basis as legal entities from EU member states. Thus, the Western Balkans are already largely integrated into Europe. Accordingly, the problem is not so much (or merely) a lack of progress in the integration process, but that in good times Europe exports prosperity to the region but in times of crisis it exports instability (Bechev, 2012). In short, not only has the EU been experiencing a profound crisis with implications for its willingness to accept new member states, but also states in the Western Balkans are displaying various degrees of Euro-scepticism.

EU diplomacy and the Western Balkans

Despite the rhetoric adopted by the European institutions, one can see a range of attitudes among the member states toward the enlargement to the Western Balkans. Some EU countries can be more favourable than others because of the benefits produced by a larger single market or for the availability of a trained workforce. However, even inside these countries, one can find debates about the repercussion of the enlargement in terms of integration of migrant workers or fear of the supposed increase of crime produced by less strict controls on the borders. So, the EU appears in its declaration much more united than it is in reality, with enlargement to the Western Balkans not only seen as a part of the EU policies of the member states but also as a salient issue for the different domestic policies of the EU member states. Furthermore, if, on the one side, it is a mistake to look at the EU member states as sharing a common position, on the other side it is also misleading not to consider the "preferences" the member states can have for entry of specific countries from the Western Balkans. For example, Slovenia and Croatia were the two countries of the ex-Yugoslavia area to enter the EU. No doubt the political and economic reforms adopted made their entrance possible. However, they also took advantage of the political conditions created among the EU member states and the support demonstrated since the beginning of the 1990s by Germany and Austria.

Particularly after Brexit, Germany is certainly the most important EU state in the enlargement process. Germany has very close relations with the Western Balkans: one and a half million of its inhabitants originate from that region, German entrepreneurs are particularly active in the Western Balkans, and Germany is a huge aid donor. However, Germany is also the proponent of the strictest conditionality applied to the accessing states. Thus, Germany is at the same time the closest friend of the Western Balkans, but also the fiercest defender of the integrity of the EU. This peculiarity can be traced back to domestic policy-making: if the enlargement policy is in the hands of the federal government, the German Bundestag has the power to influence it, reinforcing the politicisation of the German position: the Bundestag has the right to deliver an opinion on decisions relating to the opening of negotiations on any country's accession to the EU.

This is evident even in the position of Germany toward Albania's accession. In September 2019, for example, the German Bundestag approved a decision shared with the Federal Government on the application of the Republic of Albania for accession to the European Union and on the recommendation made by the European Commission and the High Representative on 29 May 2019 that accession negotiations be opened (Bundestag.de, 2019). More specifically, the German Bundestag subordinated all new negotiations to the adoption of the following reforms: (I) a new electoral law; (II) the implementation of the ongoing judicial reform and functioning of the Constitutional Court and the Supreme Court; (III) proper functioning of the Special Anti-Corruption and Organised Crime Structure (SPAK); (IV) the stepping up the fight against corruption, organised crime, and money laundering; (V) tangible progress in administrative reform, including a review of the attitudes of high-ranking officials and directors; (VI) a decision of the Constitutional Court, on the legality of the local elections of 30 June 2019.

France has traditionally supported the Western Balkans' entrance into the EU because it has always seen it as an opportunity to extend its influence and power in the region. However, fewer people from the Western Balkans live in France and the issue is not particularly relevant in the French political debates. So, France recently decided to leave any initiative on this question to Germany and the UK (until Brexit). At the same time, France is also preoccupied with the integrity of the European project. At least, this is the reason declared by the French President Emanuel Macron for opposing the opening of the accession talks with North Macedonia and Albania in October 2019. As discussed, President Macron made this decision for two reasons: he subordinated any future enlargement to, first of all, reform of the EU institutions and policies, and, second, to the adoption of adequate domestic mechanisms to prevent any subsequent democratic backsliding, such as those happening in Hungary. In an attempt to react to the inevitable criticisms, in November 2019 the French Government published a non-paper entitled "reversibility needed in new enlargement strategy", suggesting the need for "A renewed approach to the accession process (…) to support the Western Balkan countries in concrete terms with regard to the reforms necessary to fully comply with the rule of law and generally to apply the European acquis" (Politico 2019). To this aim, France proposed a seven-phase process. The phases were: (i) rule of law and fundamental rights; (ii) education and research; (iii) employment and social affairs; (iv) financial affairs; (v) the single market, agriculture, and fish; (vi) foreign affairs; and (vii) "other matters" which would form coherent blocs of policies. The previously recalled European Commission's Communication on "Enhancing the accession process - A credible EU perspective for the Western Balkans" adopted in 2020 is strongly influenced by the French non-paper. It states, "A core objective of the European Union's engagement with the Western Balkans is to prepare them to meet all the requirements of membership. This includes supporting fundamental democratic, rule of law and economic reforms and alignment with core European values. This will in turn foster solid and accelerated economic growth and social convergence" (European Commission ND).

Historically, the UK had been at the forefront of efforts to enlarge the EU. The main reason for the British position was its opposition to any possible development toward the transformation of the EU from an economic to a political union. The UK, in other words, tried to use the EU enlargement as a way to prevent any EU deepening: the general assumption was that the more complex the EU, the less possibility there is for the creation of a federal union. For this reason, particularly in the 1990s and in the 2000s, the UK took the lead in the negotiations and appeared to be the most enthusiastic EU member in terms of opening the borders to the freedom of movement, particularly after the 2004 enlargement. However, the number of migrants going to the UK from Central and Eastern Europe was far above the figures imagined by the British governments and fuelled Euroscepticism and populism in British politics thus paving the way (among other factors) to the Brexit referendum. Therefore, not only did British enthusiasm rapidly vanish in 2010, but also the decision to leave the EU relegated the UK to a marginal role in any decision related to the future of the Western Balkans. Nowadays, the relations between the UK and the Western Balkans are mainly downgraded to bilateral agreements, such as the Trade Agreement with Albania on deepening economic relationships signed in Tirana in February 2021. Quite paradoxically, when the UK tries to be more influential, it has to involve the EU Special Representative to the Western Balkans, as happened in the occasion of the Meeting between the UK Foreign Secretary and the Western Balkans Six (WB6) Foreign Ministers on 13 December 2021 in London.

The Western Balkans enlargement constitutes a major challenge also for Central and Eastern European countries. Among them, Hungary deserves a special mention for its geographical position and the decisions taken during the migration crisis in 2015. Unlike the UK, Hungary has historically supported the entrance of the Western Balkans into the EU because of its extensive and deeply rooted cultural links. Domestic factors also played a role in this position: Hungary has always instrumentally used its position as an EU member for obtaining stricter legislation for the protection of Hungarian minorities living in the Western Balkans, especially in Serbia. However, the illiberal turn imposed by the Hungarian Prime Minister Viktor Orbán produced a marginalization of the country in the EU, making its support for enlargement less influential. Moreover, during the 2015 migration crisis, with many migrants trying to enter Europe from the Balkans, Hungary decided to close its boundaries incrementing the pressure on Slovenia and Croatia.

However, the ambiguities of many EU member states toward the Western Balkans are well represented by Greece. On the one hand, Greece rhetorically declares its strong support for the inclusion of the whole region into the EU, even in periods of enlargement fatigue. On the other hand, it is also an obstructing player, particularly when its multiple interests in the Balkans produce friction towards candidates with whom Athens has disputes. After initially blocking Albania, the publicised dispute with Macedonia over its name is but another example. Three key factors help understand the Greek position: the particularities of Greece's foreign policy-making; the background of Greece's relationship with the region and the legacy of multiple disputes created or exacerbated in the early post-Communist period; and lastly the 1990s legacy of turning EU enlargement policy into a Greek foreign policy tool. As written by Ker-Lindsay and colleagues "In many ways, Greece is the clearest example of how an EU member state has instrumentalized enlargement to secure its national interests and foreign policy goals" (Ker-Lindsay, Armakolas, Balfour, & Stratulat, 2017: 511).

Photo 16: Tito
Licence: Public domain,
Wikipedia Commons.

Photo 17: Mao Zedong and Enver Hoxha, 1956
License: Public domain, Wikipedia Commons.

Photo 19: Operazione Pellicano. La medaglia commemorativa dell'operazione Pellicano creata dall'esercito italiano
Licence: Public domain, Wikipedia Commons.

Photo 18: Nave Valona
Licence: Agjencia Telegrafike Shqiptare.

Photo 20: Visit of José Manuel Barroso, President of the EC, to Albania. License: © European Union, 2014

Photo 21: Press statement by President Von der Leyen with Prime Minister Fiala, Prime Minister Rama and Prime Minister Kovachevski on the start of the accession negotiations process and of the screening of the EU acquis.
License: © European Union, 2022

7

Western Balkans: In the "waiting room" for EU membership?

Engaging with the Western Balkans in their quest to join the EU and be closer to Europe has been a desire for some time. For the Western Balkan nations this wait has been very long. A specific German initiative known as the Berlin Process (also known as the "Connectivity Agenda"), was launched by Chancellor Angela Merkel in 2014. Initially, this process sought to link the Western Balkans Six (WB6) countries – Serbia, Albania, Bosnia and Herzegovina (BiH), Macedonia, Montenegro and Kosovo, in areas of transport and energy, and later expand into other areas such as youth exchanges and economic connections. It was a specific attempt to facilitate the four EU freedoms, namely capital, trade, people, and services through regional co-operation between WB6 countries. It was an exercise to better prepare the WB6 for EU membership. Despite its good intentions, the Berlin Process remained a German initiative which did not attract further interest. While many summits across Europe were organised since its inception in 2014 and helped to improve communication between Balkans leaders, many crucial issues remain unresolved. An initiative which stopped there.

In 2019 another initiative baptised "Mini Schengen" and then "Open Balkans" was initiated by the leaders of the three Western Balkan countries, the Serbian President, the Albanian and North Macedonian Prime Ministers. The other three of the WB6 did not participate in this initiative. Kosovo is still the main opponent of this initiative and its leaders refuse to sit and discuss with Serbian leaders without first being recognised by them. The dysfunctional parliament of BiH is unable to decide whether to join Open Balkans or not. After the pro-Serbian government of Krivokapic in Montenegro lost its legitimacy in April 2022, the new Prime Minister Abazovic reversed their opposition and is supporting the Open Balkans talks. Moreover, the Kosovar President, Vjosa Osmani expressed disappointment with Abazovic, himself an ethnic Albanian, and with the Albanian government that has supported the Open Balkans from the outset.

The Covid response and the Russian invasion of Ukraine – a new responsive EU?

After the first miss steps by the EU during the COVID-19 pandemic where the European Union acted as separate states in competition with each other, the EU, initially through the voice of the Commission President Von der Leyen, soon recovered and began demonstrating decision making tendencies more akin to a single nation state than an agglomeration of states. Its initial disregard for the out-of-control COVID spread in Italy was soon met with a *mea culpa* from Von der Leyen. On behalf of the EU, Von der Leyen apologised to Italy for its callous and insensitive response to their plight and when instead of acting with European unity she acknowledged that it was everybody for themselves. This apology soon began to reverberate throughout the EU and what followed was greater coordination in the EU over the access and distribution of protective equipment and the production of vaccinations. The EU was quick to secure 2.3 billion vaccine dozes, medical equipment for its members and Western Balkans, and create a common fund of 100 billion Euros to support unemployment, risk and emergency, as mentioned in the SURE program website:

> It can provide financial assistance up to €100 billion in the form of loans from the EU to affected Member States to address sudden increases in public expenditure for the preservation of employment. SURE, is a crucial element of the EU's comprehensive strategy to protect citizens and mitigate the severely negative socio-economic consequences of the coronavirus pandemic (European Council SURE website, 2022).

But the more historic challenge to the European Union was coming. After numerous warnings with Russian troops amassed along the Ukrainian border, Russia invaded Ukraine on 24 February 2022. This military operation sent shock waves to many, especially in Europe with realising the ramifications of this military operation. Europe and the US began imposing sanctions on Russia and calling for a halt to the invasion. In the meantime, many NATO members began shipping aid and weapons to Ukraine in the first instance. The US supported the call by the EU to offer to provide Ukraine with weaponry to repel the Russian invasion. For the first time in its history, the EU was acting almost as a nation-state – conflict against another nation state. The EU's multiple response to Russia's invasion of Ukraine included a platform of refugee protection, humanitarian, financial, civil protection, reconstruction, technical, economic assistance, and the investigation and prosecution of war crimes. As the sanctions continued, the question of Russian energy exports arose, and numerous European governments stopped or severely reduced their dependence on Russian energy sources. While producing internal difficulties, the EU urged member states to tolerate the sacrifice. Although all EU member states denounced the Russian invasion, the economies of 27 countries had various level of dependency on Russian gas and oil. This was shown to be a very sensitive matter which required careful and delicate negotiating from the EU Commission and Council.

The COVID and Ukraine events have highlighted a side of the

European Union not often demonstrated. The Von der Leyen leadership is one of the more determined leaderships of the Commission seen within the EU in years. This approach by Von der Leyen has some of the qualities of making up for the institutional inadequacies and inconclusive consultation. With the exception of Victor Orban, Hungary's Prime Minister, most of Von der Leyen's calls have been heeded by the member states and only nuances of differences have been heard. This has been especially in the case of opposition to Russia and the approach to take toward Ukraine.

Ukraine requests to join the EU …and NATO?

On 28 February 2022, shortly after Ukraine was invaded by Russia, Ukraine applied for membership of the European Union. Ukrainian President Volodymyr Zelensky requested immediate admission under a "new special procedure", and the presidents of eight EU states called for an accelerated accession process. In their bid to show support for Ukraine, and as a way to annoy Russian attempts at destroying Ukraine, Von der Leyen indicated that the EU had open arms towards Ukraine's membership and projected a fast-track option. But this dual standard for membership, while expedient for a show of support for Ukraine by the EU Commission, simultaneously upset those in the membership "waiting room". This included the Western Balkans nations. It also raised other questions for the candidate countries who were adhering to the due process of reforms and compliance of EU membership protocols. On the other hand, fast-tracking Ukraine may allow for a "faster tracking" Western Balkans for EU membership. Not likely! Clearly the offer of fast-tracking Ukraine's membership was a political choice made by the EU and more a response against Russia. Equally there is the possibility that despite all the fanfare and promises made to Ukraine, its EU membership could follow the long and fatigue road like that of the Western Balkans.

Clearly the Enlargement policy is deeply challenged by these events and throws a cat among the pigeons. While talks with Albania and North Macedonia for membership have not even started, due to a Bulgarian veto, negotiations with Serbia and Montenegro are at a standstill ever since they became candidates. Kosovo and Bosnia and Herzegovina have not even officially reached candidate status.

The Ukraine invasion has made clear to the European Union, and especially the Commission that the EU needs processes and executive powers which allow ways of responding to world events quicker and with more decisive outcomes. While reform of the EU pursues more traditional paths such as Constitutions, Treaties or other conventions, the events in Ukraine have raised the stakes in terms of decision making. Some of these nuances are as a result of the personalities such as Von der Leyen who provides strong and outspoken leadership but a challenge such as the Ukraine crisis provides the perfect occasion for this decisiveness to be addressed. It also raises the question of a European defence force which does not carry the baggage and history of NATO. When it comes to the security issue, the EU cannot militarily defend any of its countries as the entire EU security landscape is built around NATO meaning significant US involvement.

Pro-Russian ambiguity in the Western Balkans

As opposed to Western Europe, the Western Balkans is a location where Russia has loyalties of historic nature. Partially through the historically close Serbian-Russian orthodox brotherhood links and only significant pressure did Serbia denounce Russia's acts in Ukraine. Moreover, Serbia and Bosnia-Herzegovina are the only European countries that have not placed sanctions on Russia which would indicate that some of the Western Balkans have options other than the European Union. This is challenging for the EU.

Croatia, Albania, North Macedonia, Kosovo and Montenegro

have all supported the condemnation of Russia and supported sanctions against it. These are countries that are in substance all pro-EU and NATO, so is the Muslim and Croatian part of Bosnia and Montenegro. However, the other side of the Bosnian triangle – Republika Srpska through its leader, Milorad Dodik, fully supports the Russian position and thus, aligns with Serbian policies. Therefore, the Bosnian ethnic-triangle is again in danger of destruction from three main actors: Bosnian Croats, Bosnian-Muslims and Bosnian Serbs. What has emerged is the potential for the Ukrainian war to provide ongoing aftershocks in the Western Balkans.

As a small and vulnerable country with a composition of nearly 30% ethnic Serbs, Montenegro is directly affected by Serbian policies. The current government coalition led by the leader of the 'Black and White' party, Abazovic has replaced the pro-Serbian government, to which Abazovic was part of. Although the current Montenegrin government is continuing to maintain the EU and NATO alliance, historical, political and economic dependencies on Serbia are always present. As a result, Abazovic's government is very fragile.

Although the current North Macedonian government has clearly sided with the EU and NATO, its previous pro-Russian supporters are in large numbers and the official position could turn. The effects of the Ukrainian war are also felt deeply in Kosovo. The unresolved business with Serbia is making Kosovo no less vulnerable to Bosnia and Herzegovina. Kosovo can only protect its territory from Serbia and Russia through its only choice of appealing to both, the EU and NATO. It is the anxiety from Serbia and the current opposition from Russia which is fuelling fear amongst Kosovar leadership and thereby calling for immediate NATO membership and a NATO permanent military base in its territory. Similar to Kosovo's approach, Albania seems to have a more consolidated position against Russia and thus supports the sanctions against Russia. Although Albania's NATO membership is believed to place security concerns to rest, the EU membership fatigue is turning to frustration.

An alternative to EU membership... Associate membership?

It has been clear that in the last decade the integration process has been shelved. It seems to be easy for the Western Balkan countries to blame the EU for postponing the enlargement process, whereas the EU is keep rising the bar. Europe has dealt with recessions, migration crisis, and the ongoing effects of the global pandemic, however, issues of identity has always been central to European values. After some disappointment with Eastern countries and their economies, the EU is now looking closer to Western Balkan countries' performance.

However, some democratic challenges forced the EU leaders in finding a solution for Western Balkans. In 2019, French president Emmanuel Macron stated that "the EU made a collective mistake declaring the EU membership as our only relationship with the Western Balkans" (Antic 2022). Upon this call the EU introduced a revised enlargement methodology, which only allows candidates to draw financial benefits to only areas they have made progress. Should a candidate state bad perform they would never pass a key threshold, and thus, never join the EU.

Balkan countries stuck in this limbo of a perpetual process would become part of what could be considered the EU's newfound strategic vision: instead of members, a group of EU associate states (Antic 2022). According to this concept, Western Balkan countries can secure a relative stability while they are part of the block, but not members. They can develop their own economy and infrastructure based on prescribed policies. In short, they will not be part of the political decisions of the block, whereas defence security will be guaranteed by NATO. This project may bring to an end Serbia's position of sitting on two chairs, but the practical implementation of associated EU members project remains an open question.

What prospects for the Western Balkans and the European Union coming together?

Despite many cultural similarities of the nations within the Western Balkans it remains to this day a place of deeply felt ethnic divisions. While tensions between Croatia and Serbia persist, they are believed to be at least dormant for the moment. With such a legacy two are the imminent challenges in the Western Balkans: The unity and existence of Bosnia and Herzegovina and the agreement between Serbia and Kosovo. On the one hand, Republika Srbska through its leader, Dodik has little interest in aligning with the EU and is more drawn to Serbia and Russia. The danger of shifting borders in the Western Balkans is real after Dodik's claims of separating from BiH and uniting with Serbia. Serbia is also hoping to keep alive their hopes of including Kosovo as part of their territory. The leaders in Belgrade and Dodik can only count on the leverage and power of Russia to achieve their aims. Some observers fear that it would take very little to see the Western Balkans return the years of ethnic rivalry and tensions unable to overcome ethnic and religious differences all soaked in poverty and a scarcity of economic wellbeing. Others believe that countries such as Albania, Kosovo and B&H are lacking the political will to transform the enthusiasm of their population in joining the EU through real reforms (Belloni 2022: 168). Nevertheless, regardless of the will of their political elites, it is a fact that the Euro-optimism for Albanians and Kosovars has remained steady and above 80 percent – higher than perhaps any European country, whereas according to the 2018 data, in the last decade, the desire to join the EU for the people of North Macedonia, Montenegro, B&H and Serbia, has dropped to respectively 59%; 53%; 45% and 29% (Belloni 2022: 165). With Serbian population being at the bottom of the Euro-optimism, it is not hard to realise that Serbs living in B&H are affecting the entire country's desire to join the EU, bringing it down to 45% from 75% in 2010. In short, although anecdotal, the analyses show that ethnic Serbs are not very optimistic of joining the EU, and thus for them the alternative is Russia.

What this study has told us is that the Albanian journey through history has been filled with disappointments and unachieved objectives. The period since the end of the Hoxha rule has not produced the benefits many thought it would. Albania remains in search of a geo-political home and embracing the Euro-Atlantic path while abandoning the East (Xhaferi 2020) will remain a challenge. It is surrounded by benefactors who have used it for their own needs but ultimately see little value in it. Much of this feeling is felt by ordinary Albanians and to some extent by the weak Albanian political elite.

At the institutional level, Italy had little in the way of a specific foreign policy towards Albania. During the 1980s Italy made additional efforts to undermine the Hoxha regime, but these efforts were less effective than their neighbours in the West. While Italian TV came to have an important role in Albania only circumstantially, for years, American, British and German efforts engaged in informational campaigns in Albania with the broadcasting of media programs such as Voice of America, Radio Free Europe, BBC Albanian service, Deutsche Welle and the like with an aim at undermining the Albanian communist government.

While former Italian prime minister Draghi has made clear that Albanian membership of the EU is important in his speech before the European Parliament he mentioned that "Italy supports the immediate opening of membership negotiations with Albania and Northern Macedonia, in accordance with the decision taken by the European Council in March 2020", this view has not taken on much weight (Politiko 2022a). This Italian view is more tempered by the fact that Italy has lost much interest in Albania and has gladly let other nations, including the European Union to take the lead. In the aftermath of the collapse of Albania, Italian foreign policy towards Albania was ambivalent: partially it was a place of interest but partially it provided more problems than benefits. The reason for this change of heart is largely that Italy sees Albania no longer as an economic benefit but a security risk some of which is reflected in the flight of its population which lands up on Italian shores. As was clear, Italy saw more opportunity and interest in a least likely ally in Serbia despite the difficulty in befriending it and controlling its historic legacy and allies.

Recent research from the European Council on Foreign Relations (ECFR) asserts that "while Europeans feel great solidarity with Ukraine and support sanctions against Russia, they are split about the long-term goals. They divide between a "Peace" camp (35 per cent of people) that wants the war to end as soon as possible, and a "Justice" camp that believes the more pressing goal is to punish Russia (25 per cent of people)" (ECFR 2022).

Decision making and the Veto system

It has been argued that the integration process is not as deep as it should be, and that the EU's political structure and status is far from being a federal in its nature. The Western Balkan integration is not the only example that has shown signs of disagreements between member states. Although it seems premature to question the EU unity and its effectiveness, the veto regime needs to be considered. Often, we have seen single countries block EU projects, if they are considered to be against their own local, national and very narrow agendas. Examples of Greece blocking Albania's and North Macedonia's accessions are now followed by Bulgaria's veto on North Macedonia due to the ethnic identity issues. The EU is entrenched in its consensus approach and the use of the veto (by one-member state) is beginning to wear thin. It is only a matter of time before there is a move towards majority consensus in order for decisions to be made and to avoid the power of a single member state to exert such influence on EU outcomes.

The new tasks facing the European Union provoked by COVID and the Russian invasion of Ukraine make clear that the EU has major reforms itself to undertake. Its behaviour in the Ukraine events saw it play the role of a "united state" with a clear agenda and working its agenda over time. Its approach towards these events did not see it play a passive role, leaving the voice of Europe to be made by the single member states. This time it is the EU taking the lead – right or wrong – which we are not used to seeing. This of course raises important scenarios about how the EU will need to change in the future. Accepting new members may not be important as it was and the concern about drafting the Western Balkans appears to be one of hesitancy and more likely stalling. The EU may have realised it has made a mistake and is unsure how to step back. Equally the tolerance level of vetoes by a single nation over an issue of regional irritation will be heavily scrutinised and many in the EU will be looking for reforms which will supersede this behaviour. Whether it is Hungary on matters related to Russian sanctions or Bulgaria vetoing North Macedonia for historic border issues – the EU will be seeking institutional solutions to this behaviour in order to be able to function as a united entity.

Other variants in the Albanian political direction

The rise of the European Union as one of the multipolar political players provides a new actor and one which has received much attention in Albania. The task of entering the orbit of the European Union has been a difficult one and to this day might remain elusive for Albania. Given Albania's poverty, corruption and lack of political democracy, it is unlikely that Albania will ever satisfy the EU criteria. Much might depend on the political necessity of having Albania within the European Union. Each side in this equation however has a sense of purpose and self-respect and the Albanian political elites may turn their back on membership and create or identify workable partners.

While the entry of Turkey into the EU was clearly a political problem under Erdogan, the EU is hoping for better times in Turkey's internal political dynamics. In short many are waiting for when Erdogan eventually goes. The economics of the Western Balkans looked quite bleak and the toying with new categories of membership of the EU seems to be the political overlay for legitimising an arm's length membership with certain countries. However, what is raised with the possible EU membership of Turkey is the religious factor. While the EU will brush off such an insinuation that religion plays a role in being compatible with the European Union, it nonetheless is felt by those quarters, such as Albania that being Muslim is not helping its chances.

Much of the consternation around the direction of the EU, its size and objectives are determined around what it is and seeks to be. There are many views on this, and its course remains undecided. Largely this is due to outside geopolitical factors as well as the political dynamics of European politics. The rise of right-wing, anti-EU governments should not be excluded and another four years of the return of Trumpism in the White House provides little certainty for the EU and its ability to place itself as a global leader. What appears to be certain is that new members to the EU from the Western Balkans have the smell of more trouble than solutions.

Another actor on the scene is the economically powerful China which has received far too little attention. Despite being ambivalent about the Russian invasion in Ukraine and indirectly not wishing to line up with the West, China is a far greater player even on the European landscape that what is thus far acknowledged. This is primarily because China believes in economic growth and economic expansion. This has to include even more expansion into Europe especially given the closed doors in North America and elsewhere. While China will not engage in the provision of mass Chinese products as was the case in the last two decades, China's investment and technology development plans are ambitious. Especially given the slow demise of the US as the global superpower, and its declining economic prowess, Europe and the Western Balkans should ready themselves for more China and not less. In terms of the Western Balkans, China has already offered the Belt and Road (BIR) infrastructure investment projects which are having a major impact in Greece and Serbia. Would a country like Albania jump at the opportunity to be part of the BIR which is far more concrete rather than the promises coming from the EU? Or would the Tirana leadership be loyal to their strategical choice such as the Euro-Atlantic path? The political elites in Albania have more than once demonstrated that their loyalty is as strong as the dollars that are thrown at it and that they can be easily bought. Moreover, Albania has so little going for it that it would take very little for it to enjoy small pickings of big projects. Their loyalty to Western alliances for the sake of ideology and value systems is difficult to believe. Nevertheless, remaining in NATO for Albania is primarily to find security from capricious neighbours who at the drop of a hat would seek to eat into Albanian territory. Once the security dilemma is resolved, Albanians may easily replace the appetite of joining the EU. The Albanian political elite repeat the same postulate that there is no alternative for Albania than the path to the EU. And there is of course around the corner Turkey – the regional power that never hesitates to support Albania while sharing the pain regarding Europe's continuous rejections.

Closing remarks

In late June 2022 the EU Council addressed the question of Ukraine (and Georgia and Moldova) membership of the EU. In their concluding media release, point number 11 of the declaration stated: "The European Council has decided to grant the status of candidate country to Ukraine and to the Republic of Moldova" (European Council 2022). It further stipulated in clause 14 that "The progress of each country towards the European Union will depend on its own merit in meeting the Copenhagen criteria, taking into consideration the EU's capacity to absorb new members" (European Council 2022).

In a meeting with the EU leadership on 24 June 2022 the Western Balkan leaders were again disappointed by a non-committal EU to their membership bid. The Western Balkans have seen their EU bid for EU membership yet again hit a wall, with dwindling prospects of a significant breakthrough (Chadwick & Liboreiro, 2022). Alongside the Bulgarian veto of North Macedonia's opening of membership discussion, Albania through its Prime Minister Rama, was furious at the perceived weakness of the EU in the handling this case. German MEP Von Cramon made no secret of the failure of the European Union before the leaders of the Western Balkans visit to Brussels:

> This summit for the Western Balkans was a complete failure. I have to admit that I am terribly disappointed and when the Commission called itself a geopolitical commission, come on, this is a joke. Look: They let them travel to Brussels, all six, and they were not given anything, they were not given anything. Bosnia has not received candidate status either, worse yet, Northern Macedonia and Albania did not receive accession negotiations and Kosovo did not receive visa liberalization, an issue that has been dragging on for four years now.
> This is indeed a catastrophic signal (Politiko 2022b).

It is unlikely that the events facing Europe and the Western Balkans will provide Albania the assurance that it is seeking in its drive for a political and economic home. Years of delay and pockets of open resistance and opposition to Albania joining the EU might send a message that no one should have their hopes up. In addition, Albanian expectations of what membership of the EU will mean might also be over expected. Like Croatia in 2013, many thought that membership of the EU would provide countless economic benefits which was wildly exaggerated. Albania has some of the same illusions.

While the EU maintains its traditional wall of reserve, pursuing the irreverent institutional approach, the Ukraine crisis tells us that the EU is equally opportunist in seeking political outcomes for its betterment and for it to be a global actor with teeth. To many elites in the EU the Western Balkans seems like a bag of unwanted political and ethnic problems which would only drag the whole EU backwards. Moreover, the entry of more countries that are primarily rural without economic sophistication of western economies compounds many of the EUs own deficiencies. This was one of the experiences of the 2004 enlargement towards the East.

Fundamentally Albania and to a similar extent, the Western Balkans, is not the owner of its destination. For more than a century, Albania has mostly acted within a framework created by the decisions of the "Great Powers" of yesterday and today. The geopolitical stand-off involving the US, China, the EU and Russia make Albania again a receiver of a political destiny. Moreover, it is a country in a region fraught with rival neighbours and a diaspora which is dispersed and volatile. Kosovo being the point here. It is unlikely that the immediate period before us will produce any major change in Albania's political direction and Albania will need to wait again for a more favourable moment in history to find its political home and lasting identity.

Bibliography

Amato, G. 2005, Forward, in International Commission on the Balkans, The Balkans in Europe's Future, Robert Bosch Stiftungiking, Baudouin Foundation, German Marshall Fund of the United States & Charles Stewart Mott Foundation, Sofia, pp. 3-4.

Antić, S. 2022, In the Balkans, the EU Wants Associates, Not Members, The National Interest, 3 February, https://nationalinterest.org/blog/buzz/balkans-eu-wants-associates-not-members-200313, Viewed 25 August 2022.

B92.net. 2014, Unconditional Withdrawal of Genocide Lawsuits, 8 January, https://www.b92.net/eng/news/politics.php?yyyy=2014&mm=01&dd=08&nav_id=88911, Viewed 25 August 2022.

Balfour, R., Stratulat, C. (eds). 2015, EU member states and enlargement towards the Balkans, European Policy Centre, Issue Paper No. 79, Brussels.

Baltsiotis, L. 2011, The Muslim Chams of Northwestern Greece. The grounds for the expulsion of a "non-existent" minority community, European Journal of Turkish Studies. Social Sciences on Contemporary Turkey, Vol. 12, https://journals.openedition.org/ejts/4444, Viewed 28 August 2022.

Bartlett, W. & Prica, I. 2013, The deepening crisis in the European super-periphery, Journal of Balkan and Near Eastern Studies, Vol. 15, No. 4, pp. 367–82.

Bassuener, K.& Weber, B. 2013, House of Cards: The EU's "Reinforced Presence" in Bosnia and Herzegovina. Proposal for a new policy approach, Democratization Policy Council, Berlin.

Batir, B. 2012, Case of Italy-Albania relations: Policy cultural interaction (1878-1918), International Balkan Annual Conference, vol.1, pp. 110–23, http://dspace.epoka.edu.al/handle/1/304, Viewed 25 August 2022.

Bechev, D. 2012, The Periphery of the periphery: the Western Balkans and the Euro Crisis. European Council on Foreign Relations, London.

Belloni, R. 2009, European integration and the Western Balkans: lessons, prospects and obstacles, Journal of Balkan and Near Eastern Studies, Vol. 11, No. 3, pp. 313–31.

Belloni, R. 2014, L'euroscepticisme croissant des Balkans occidentaux, La Revue Nouvelle, Vol. 6, pp. 18–23.

Belloni, R. 2022, I Balcani dopo le guerre: Ascesa e declino dell'intervento internazionale, Carocci, Roma.

Belloni, R., Kappler, S. & Ramovic, J. 2016, Bosnia-Herzegovina: Domestic agency and the inadequacy of the liberal peace», in S. Pogodda & O.P. Richmond (eds.), Post-liberal peace transitions: Between peace formation and state formation, Edinburgh University Press, Edinburg, pp. 47–64.

Ben-Ghiat, R. & Fuller, M. 2008, Italian colonialism, Palgrave Macmillan, London.

Bianchi, V. 2018, Carlo Sforza and Diplomatic Europe 1896-1922, Unpublished PhD Thesis, Università La Sapienza, Roma.

Biberaj, E. 1985, Albania After Hoxha: Dilemmas of Change, Problems of Communism, Vol. 34, No. 6, pp. 32–47.

Bogdani, M. & Loughlin, J.P. 2007, Albania and the European Union: the tumultuous journey towards integration and accession, IB Tauris London.

Börzel, T.A. 2013, When Europeanization hits limited statehood: The Western Balkans as a test case for the transformative power of Europe, in A. Elbasani (ed.), European integration and transformation in the Western Balkans, Routledge, London, pp. 173-184.

Bufacchi V. & Burgess S., 2001, Italy since 1989, Events and Interpretations, Houndmills, Palgrave, UK.

Capps, E. 1963, Greece, Albania, and Northern Epirus, Argonaut, London.

Cervi, M. 1971, *The hollow legions: Mussolini's blunder in Greece, 1940-1941*, Doubleday, Garden City.

Chadwick, L. & Liboreiro, J. 2022, "You Are a Mess Guys": Albania PM Angry over EU Membership Delays, Euronews, 23 June, https://www.euronews.com/my-europe/2022/06/23/you-are-a-mess-guys-albania-pm-angry-over-eu-membership-delays, Viewed 25 August 2022.

Chiodi, L. & Devole, R. 2006, Conflicting memories and mutual representations: Italy and Albania since 1989, Osservatorio Balcani e Caucaso, Occasional Paper, January, https://www.balcanicaucaso.org/content/download/77872/663213/version/12/file/Download+-++Conflicting+memories+and+mutual+representations.Italy+and+Albania+since+1989.pdf, Viewed 25 August 2022.

Ciano G., 1952, Ciano's diary 1937-38, Methuen & Co. London.

Council of the European Union, 1999, 'Presidency Conclusions', Cologne European Council Meeting, 3-4 June 1999

Council of the European Union, 2000, 'Presidency Conclusions', Santa Maria de Feira European Council Meeting, 19-20 June 2000, Press Release Nr: 2000/1/00

Crnobrnja, M. 1994, The Yugoslav Drama. McGill-Queen's University Press, Montreal.

Czekalski, T. 2013, The shining beacon of socialism in Europe: the Albanian state and society in the period of communist dictatorship 1944-1992, Jagiellonian University Press, Kraków.

Dervishi, K. 2006, Albanian State History 1912-2005. State organization, political life, key events, all legislators, ministers and presidents swear state, Publishing House 55, Tirana.

Durham, M.E. (July/December 1919), 'Albania and Powers', Contemporary Review, (119).

ECFR European Council on Foreign Relations, 2022, Peace versus Justice: The coming European split over the war in Ukrainehttps://ecfr.eu/publication/peace-versus-justice-the-coming-european-split-over-the-war-in-ukraine/, 15 June 2022, viewed 21 June 2022.

Economides, S. & J. Ker-Lindsay 2015, Pre-Accession Europeanization: The Case of Serbia and Kosovo, Journal of Common Market Studies, Vol. 53, No. 5 (2015), pp. 1027-44.

Eurobarometer 2015, 'Public Opinion in the European Union', Standard Eurobarometer 83, July, http://ec.europa.eu/public_-opinion/archives/eb/eb83/eb83_first_en.pdf, Viewed 25 August 2022.

Eurobarometer, 2011, Public Opinion in the European Union, Standard Eurobarometer 74, February, http://ec.europa.eu/public_opinion/archives/eb/eb74/eb74_publ_en.pdf, Viewed 25 August 2022.

European Commission, 2003, The Thessaloniki Summit: a milestone in the European Union's relations with the Western Balkans, Press release Ip/03/860, Brussels, 18 June.

European Commission, 2005, Eurobarometer 63: Public opinion in the European Union, September.

European Commission, 2006, Enlargement Strategy and Main Challenges 2006-2007, COM (2006) 649, Brussels, 8 November.

European Commission, 2010, Staff Working Paper, Albania 2010 Progress Report, Brussels: 9 November 2010, COM (2010) 680.

European Commission, 2012, Enlargement Strategy and Main Challenges 2012-2013, Brussels, 10.10.2012, COM (2012) 600.

European Commission, 2014, Staff Working Paper, Albania 2014 Progress Report, Brussels: 8.10.2014, COM (2014) 700.

European Commission, 2020, Communication from the Commission to the European Parliament, the Council, the European Economic and Social Committee and the Committee of the Regions, Enhancing the accession process - A credible EU perspective for the Western Balkans, Brussels, 5.2.2020 COM(2020) 57 final.

European Commission, ND, https://ec.europa.eu/neighbourhood-enlargement/document-/download/ef0547a9-c063-4225-b1b4-93ff9027d0c0_en?filename=enlargement-methodology_en.pdf

European Council, 2022, The European instrument for temporary Support to mitigate Unemployment Risks in an Emergency (SURE), , https://ec.europa.eu/info/business-economy-euro/economic-and-fiscal-policy-coordination/financial-assistance-eu/funding-mechanisms-and-facilities/sure_en, Viewed 29 June 2022.

European Stability Initiative, 2005, 'The Helsinki Moment: European Member-State Building in the Balkans', https://www.esiweb.org/pdf/esi_document_id_65.pdf, Viewed 26 August 2022.

European Stability Initiative, 2014, Vladimir and Estragon in Skopje - A fictional conversation on trust and standards and a plea on how to break a vicious circle, https://www.esiweb.org/publications/vladimir-and-estragon-skopje-fictional-conversation-trust-and-standards-and-plea-how, Viewed 26 August 2022.

Fouéré, E. 2014, Bilateral Disputes – A Dark Cloud over the Balkans, Centre for European Policy Studies, Brussels, 24 January.

Freedom House, 2014, Nations in Transit 2014: Eurasia's Rupture with Democracy, USAID, Washington, DC. https://freedomhouse.org/sites/default/files/2020-02/NIT2014%20booklet_WEBSITE.pdf, Viewed 26 August 2022.

Goxha, J. 2016, Migration in the early '90s: Italy coping with Albanian illegal emigration, European Scientific Journal, Vol. 12, No. 11, pp. 254-64.

Grabbe H., Knaus G., & Korski D. 2010, Beyond Wait-and-See: the Way Forward for EU Balkan Policy, Council on Foreign Relations, Brussels, https://ecfr.eu/wp-content/uploads/ECFR21_BALKAN_BRIEF.pdf, Viewed 27 August 2022.

Guy, N. 2008, "Ethnic nationalism, the Great powers and the question of Albanian independence, 1912-1921", Ph.D. thesis, Durham University.

Hall, R.C. 2000, The Balkan Wars 1912–1913: Prelude to the First World War, Routledge, London.

Hamm, H. 1963, Albania-China's Beachhead in Europe, Frederick A Praeger, New York.

Hodgkinson, H. (ed.) 1999, Scanderbeg, Centre for Albanian Studies, London.

Hoxha, A.R. 2017, la cortina di ferro sull'Adriatico vista dall'altro lato dell'Atlantico: L'Italia e l'Albania sotto la lente di Washington (1945-1961), in P. Rago (ed), Una pace necessaria: I rapporti italiano-albanesi nella prima fase della guerra fredda, Editori Laterza, Roma, pp. 63-94.

Hoxha, E. 1979, Reflections on China, Norman Bethune Institute, Toronto.

Hoxha, E. 1983, "Mbi gjendjen aktuale nderkombetare" [About the international situation]

Vepra 39 [volume 39], Shtepia botuese "8 Nentori", Tirana.

Hoxhaj, A. 2021, The EU Rule of Law Initiative Towards the Western Balkans, Hague Journal on the Rule of Law, Vol. 13, pp. 143-72.

Iastrides J.O. & Wringley L. (eds) 1995, Greece At The Crossroads: The Civil War and Its Legacy, Penn State University Press, University Park, PA.

Jackson, L.B.,2018, Islamophobia and National Identity in Europe, in L.B. Jackson (ed.), Islamophobia in Britain: The Making of a Muslim Enemy, Palgrave Macmillan, London, pp. 115-144.

Jarvis C., 2000 The Rise and Fall of Albania's Pyramid Schemes, Finance and Development, Vol. 37, Issue 1, https://www.imf.org/external/pubs/ft/fandd/2000/03/jarvis.htm, Viewed 22 August 2022.

Jelavich, C. & Jelavich, B. 1977, The Establishment of the Balkan National States, 1804-1920, University of Washington Press, Seattle.

Judah, T. 2009, The Serbs: History, Myth and the Destruction of Yugoslavia,

Yale University Press, New Haven.

Kadare, I. 2006, Identiteti evropian i shqiptarëve, Onufri, Tirana.

Kadare, I. 2011, Mosmarrëveshja: Mbi raportet e Shqipërisë me vetveten, Onufri, Tirana.

Ker-Lindsay J., Armakolas I., Balfour R. & Stratulat, C. 2017, The national politics of EU enlargement in the Western Balkans, Southeast European and Black Sea Studies, Vol. 17, No. 4, pp. 511-22.

Ker-Lindsay, J. 2009, Kosovo: The path to contested statehood in the Balkans, I.B. Tauris, London.

Këshilli i Ministrave 2008, Strategjia kombëtare për zhvillim dhe integrim 2007–2013, https://www.connectwitheu.al/wp-content/uploads/2019/06/Strategjia-komb%c3%abtare-p%c3%abr-zhvillim-dhe-integrim-_2008_-p%c3%abr-periudh%c3%abn-2007-2013.pdf, Viewed 27 August 2022.

Kochenov, D. 2004, Behind the Copenhagen Façade: The Meaning and Structure of the Copenhagen Political Criterion of Democracy and the Rule of Law, European Integration Online Papers, Vol. 8, No. 10, pp. 1-24.

Koleka, B. 2008, Albanian witness in U.S. arms probe dies suddenly", Reuters, https://www.reuters.com/article/us-albania-blast-witness-idUSLC14849820080912, Viewed 27 August 2022.

Kostovicova, D. 2016, Reaction to Brexit Around Europe: How the Result Affects the Balkans, LSE Blogs, https://blogs.lse.ac.uk/europpblog/2016/06/24/reaction-to-brexit-around-europe-how-the-result-affects-the-balkans/, Viewed 27 August 2022.

Leeds, C. 1974, The unification of Italy, Wayland Publishers, London.

Likmeta, B. 2011, Threat of Violence Hangs Over Albania Protest, Balkan Insight, 21 January, https://balkaninsight.com/2011/01/21/threat-of-violence-hangs-over-albania-protest/, Viewed 27 august 2022.

Limaj, H.M. 2012, Midis Ankarasë dhe Tiranës: 1990-2000. Nga ditari i një atasheu ushtarak, Emal, Tirana.

Luzaj, I. ND, Musine Kokalari, https://www.luzaylibrary.com/?s=kokalari, Viewed 27 August 2022.

Mack Smith, D. 1968, The making of Italy, 1796-1866, MacMillan, London.

Makrides V.N. 2009, Orthodox Anti-Westernism Today: A Hindrance to European Integration? International Journal for the Study of the Christian Church, Vol. 9, No. 3, pp. 209-224.

Malcolm, N. 1999, Kosovo: A Short History, New York University Press, New York.

Milekic, S. & Pantovic, M. 2016, Croatia-Serbia Tensions Escalate Into Diplomatic War, Balkan Insight, 29 July, https://balkaninsight.com/2016/07/29/croatia-serbia-tensions-escalate-into-diplomatic-war-07-29-2016/, Viewed 27 August 2022.

Ministero del Lavoro e delle politiche sociali 2020, La comunità albanese in Italia: Rapporto Annuale sulla presenza dei migranti, Roma, https://www.lavoro.gov.it/documenti-e-norme/studi-e-statistiche/Documents/Rapporti%20annuali%20sulle%20comunit%-C3%A0%20migranti%20in%20Italia%20-%20anno%202020/Albania-rapporto-2020.pdf, Viewed 27 August 2022.

Ministero della Difesa, (ND), Albania – Pellicano, Roma, https://www.esercito.difesa.it-/operazioni/operazioni_oltremare/Pagine/Albania-Pellicano.aspx, Viewed 27 August 2022.

Misha, G. 1999, The Balkans 1804-1999: Nationalism, War, and the Great Powers, Granta Books, London.

Myrdal, J. & Kessle, G. 1976, Albania Defiant, Monthly Review Press, London.

Nexhipi, A. & Nexhipi E. 2019, Albania's European Perspective and the Albanian Politics, European Journal of Multidisciplinary Studies, Vol. 4, Issue 3, pp. 37-48.

O'Brennan, J. 2013, 'Bulgarians Confront the Oligarchs', Open Democracy, 25 June, https://www.opendemocracy.net/en/bulgarians-confront-oligarchs/, Viewed 27 August 2022.

O'Brennan, J. 2014, 'On the Slow Train to Nowhere?' The European Union, 'Enlargement Fatigue' and the Western Balkans, European Foreign Affairs Review, Vol. 19, No. 2, pp. 221-41.

Panagiotou, R. 2013, The Greek Crisis as a Crisis of EU Enlargement: How will the Western Balkans be Affected? Southeast European and Black Sea Studies, Vol. 13, No. 1, pp. 89-104.

Pandelejmoni, E. 2017, Il rimpatrio degli italiani e lo stallo nelle relazioni Albania-Italia, in P. Rago (ed.), Una pace necessaria: I rapporti italiano-albanesi nella prima fase della Guerra fredda, Laterza, Roma, pp. 127-72.

Panorama on line, 2017, Tensionet/Erdogan kërcënon sërish, tregon se çfarë e pret Europën, 24 October, http://www.panorama.com.al/tensionet-erdogan-kercenon-serish-tregon-se-cfare-e-pret-evropen/, Viewed 27 August 2022.

Papadimitriou, D. & Petrov, P. 2013, State-building without Recognition: a Critical Perspective of the European Union's Strategy in Kosovo (1999-2010), in A. Elbasani (ed.), European Integration and Transformation in the Western Balkans, Routledge London, pp. 121-37.

Paxton, R. 1975, Europe in the twentieth century, Harcourt Brace Jovanovich, New York.

Pearson, O. 2004, Albania and King Zog: Independence, Republic and Monarchy, 1908-1939, The Centre for Albanian Studies, London.

Pearson, O. 2005, Albania in Occupation and War: From Fascism to Communism, 1940-1945, The Centre for Albanian Studies, London.

Pearson, O. 2006, Albania as Dictatorship and Democracy, From Isolation to Kosovo War 1946-1998, The Centre for Albanian Studies, London.

Perlmutter, T. 1998, The politics of proximity: The Italian response to the Albanian crisis, The International Migration, Vol. 32, No. 1, pp. 203-222.

Phinnemore, D. 2013, The Stabilization and Association Process: a Framework for European Union Enlargement? in A. Elbasani (ed.), European Integration and Transformation in the Western Balkans: Europeanization or Business as Usual?, Routledge, London, pp. 22-35.

Pippan, C. 2004, The Rocky Road to Europe: the EU's Stabilization and Association Process for the Western Balkans and the Principle of Conditionality, European Foreign Affairs Review, Vol. 9, No. 2, pp. 219-45.

Politico 2019, Non-Paper: Reforming the European Union accession process, November, https://www.politico.eu/wp-content/uploads/2019/11/Enlargement-nonpaper.pdf, Viewed 28 august 2022.

Politiko 2022a, Mario Draghi in the EU Parliament: Open negotiations with Albania and Northern Macedonia, 3 March, https://politiko.al/english/e-tjera/mario-draghi-ne-parlamentin-e-be-hapni-negociatat-me-shqiperine-dhe-maqe-i459179, viewed 28 August 2022.

Politiko 2022b, Von Cramon: EU summit a complete failure, catastrophic signal for Western Balkans, 25 June 2022, https://politiko.al/english/e-tjera/von-cramen-samiti-i-be-ishte-nje-deshtim-i-plote-sinjal-katastrofik-per--i462539, viewed 28 August 2022.

Potts, J. 2010, *The Ionian Islands and Epirus: A Cultural History*, Signal Books, Oxford.

Psilos, C. 2006, Albanian Nationalism and Unionist Ottomanization 1908 to 1912, Mediterranean Quarterly, Vol. 17, No. 3, pp. 26-42.

Rizinski, M. 2014, Republic of Macedonia – Back to Yugoslavia?, EurActiv, 23 January, http://www.euractiv.com/general/republic-macedonia-back-yugoslav-analysis-532978, Viewed 28 August 2022.

Rowland, B. 1972, Modern Italy, University Tutorial Press, UK.

Rredhi, G. (N.D.) 'Epika historike kushtuar Lidhjes Shqiptare të Prizrenit [Historical Epics dedicated to The Albanian Prizren League]', Aktet e Takimit Vjetor, Vëll. II, Nr. 1, Universiteti 'Eqerem Çabej', Gjirokaster, pp. 133-38.

Sedelmeier, U. 2015, Enlargement: Constituent Policy and Tool for External Governance, in Wallace, M.A. Pollack & A.R. Young (eds), Policy-Making in the European Union, Oxford University Press, Oxford, pp. 407-35.

Silber, L. & Little, A. 1997, Yugoslavia: Death of a Nation, Penguin Books, New York.

Skendi, S. 1957, Albania: East-Central Europe under the Communists, Thames & Hudson, London.

Smaci, E. 2017, Overview of Italian government's stance on Albania's withdrawal from Warsaw Treaty de facto in 1961 and de jure in 1968, Mediterranean Journal of Social Sciences, Vol. 8, No. 2, pp. 155-9.

Stavrianos, L.S. [1965] 2000, The Balkans since 1453, New York University Press, New York.

Sugar, P.F. 1977, Southeastern Europe under Ottoman Rule, 1354-1804, University of Washington Press, Seattle.

Taggart, P. & Szczerbiak, A. 2001, Parties, Positions and Europe: Euroscepticism in the EU Candidate States of Central and Eastern Europe, Sussex European Institute, Brighton.

The Irish Times, 1998, Milosevic and Berisha profit from the tragedy in Kosovo, June 18, https://www.irishtimes.com/news/milosevic-and-berisha-profit-from-the-tragedy-in-kosovo-1.164282, Viewed 28 August 2022.

Tretiak, D. 1962, The Founding of the Sino-Albanian Entente, The China Quarterly, Vol. 10, pp. 123-43.

Vachudova, M.A. 2014, EU Leverage and National Interests in the Balkans: The Puzzles of Enlargement Ten Years On, Journal of Common Market Studies, Vol. 52, No.1, pp. 122-38.

Van Meurs, W. 2003, The Next Europe: South-Eastern Europe after Thessaloniki, South East Europe Review, Vol. 6, No. 3, pp. 9-16.

Varsori, A. 2012, Italy and the end of communism in Albania 1989-1991, Cold War History, Vol. 12, No. 4, pp. 615-35.

Vickers, M. [1995] 2001, The Albanians: A Modern History, I.B. Taurus, London.

Vickers, M. & Pettifer, J. 1997, Albania: From Anarchy to a Balkan Identity, New York University Press, New York.

Vryonis, Jr S. (1969-1970), The Byzantine Legacy and Ottoman Forms, Dumbarton Oaks Papers, Vol. 23/24, pp. 251-308.

Wasti, S.T. 2016, Three Ottoman Pashas at the Congress of Berlin,1878, Middle Eastern Studies, Vol. 52, No. 6, pp. 938-52.

Wickham-Steed, H. 1927, Italy, Yugoslavia and Albania, Chatham House, The Royal; Institute of International Affairs, Vol. 6 No. 3, pp. 170-78.

Wolf, M. 2002, Europe risks destruction to widen peace and prosperity, in Financial Times, December 10.

Woods, D. 1992, The immigration question in Italy, in Ed. S. Hellman and G. Pasquino, Italian politics - A review Vol. 7, Berghahn Books, London, pp. 186-198.

Xhaferi, P. 2020, Albania: Escaping the East, Aspiring for the West, Connor Court, Brisbane.

Zickel, R.E. & Iwaskiw, W.R. (eds.) (1994), Albania: A Country Study, Library of Congress, Washington, D.C.

Zollo, D. 2002, Invoking humanity: war, law, and global order, Continuum International Publishing Group, London.

Index

Albanian, Lost Gold: 111-112

Austro-Hungary rule: 34, 36, 46, 48-49

Berisha, Sali: 112-114, 125-126

Berlin Congress: 20, 49

Berlin Wall: 3, 90, 93, 103-104, 108, 121

Berlusconi, Silvio: 114

Bosnia and Herzegovina: 3, 6, 12-14, 25, 34, 94, 97, 110-111, 116, 123, 129, 137-138, 144, 150, 159, 163-164, 166, 172

Bulgaria: 3, 7, 17, 21, 30, 33-34, 36, 62, 67, 76, 89

China: 7, 32, 77, 79-80, 83-85, 87, 146, 170-171, 173

Ciano, Count: 57-60

Craxi, Bettino: 88-89

Croatia: 3, 13, 67, 69, 93-97, 123, 137-138, 145-147, 151, 155, 163-164, 172

Epirus (North): 15, 17, 35, 37, 46, 48-49, 113

Erdogan, Tayyip: 170

France: 2, 7, 15, 24, 26-27, 31, 35-36, 45-46, 59, 61, 63, 68, 77, 88, 112, 115, 117, 140, 153

Germany: 2, 6-7, 23, 25-26, 35, 45, 47, 50, 57, 59, 62, 66-68, 73-74, 88, 94, 104, 108, 111-112, 114, 117, 138, 140, 142, 144, 152-153

Gorbachev, Mikhail: 91-92, 104

Greece: 2-4, 6, 11-12, 14-17, 21, 26, 29-30, 33-38, 40, 46-49, 59, 61-62, 66-68, 71, 73-74, 76-77, 82, 88-89, 112-113, 115, 118-119, 130, 137-138, 145, 148-149, 155, 168, 171

Hoxha, Enver: 5, 7, 63-68, 73, 75, 78-79, 82-87, 89, 103, 118, 148, 167

Kadare, Ismail: 5, 55, 86

Kokalari, Muzine: 64-67, 73

Kosovo: 3-4, 6, 12, 14, 20, 29, 36-37, 55, 60, 65, 69, 94-96, 106, 116-117, 137-139, 142, 144, 150-151, 159-160, 163-164, 166, 172-173

London Conference: 35-38, 48-49, 54

Luzaj, Isuf: 63, 65-67, 73, 102

Macedonia, now North: 3-4, 6, 12, 17, 21, 30, 33-34, 37, 67, 95, 97, 123, 136-137, 139, 141, 144-145, 147, 150, 153, 155, 159-160, 163-164, 166-169, 172

Milosevic, Slobodan: 93-97, 116-117

Montenegro: 3, 12, 14, 17, 20-21, 29, 33-34, 37, 40, 46, 67-68, 95, 136-137, 139, 144, 150, 159-160, 163-164, 166

Mussolini, Benito: 2, 45, 51-52, 55, 57, 59, 61, 64, 67, 101

NATO: 4, 5, 8, 81, 84, 105, 110-111, 117, 122-123, 129-130, 147, 150, 161-165, 171

Operation IFOR: 110-111

Operation Pelican: 106, 109-110, 115, 120

Ottomans: 6, 9, 11-18, 20, 28-30, 33-34, 119

Paris Peace Treaty: 49

Prodi, Romano: 114-115

Romania: 3, 34-35, 76, 89, 115, 120-121, 137-138, 143-144

Russia: 7-9, 12-13, 15, 17, 20, 30, 35-36, 45, 47, 49, 51-52, 92, 117, 146, 161-164, 166-168, 173

Serbia: 2-3, 4, 6, 9, 11-17, 20-21, 29-30, 33-37, 40, 47-49, 50, 61, 69, 93-95, 105, 113-114, 116-118, 123, 130, 136-139, 145-148, 150, 155, 159, 163-164, 166, 168, 171

Stalin, Joseph: 7, 71, 79, 81, 83

The Porte: 12, 16-20, 27-29

Tito, Broz: 69, 71-72, 74, 81, 93, 95, 156

Treaty of San Stefano: 17, 20

Turkey: 26, 30-32, 55, 82, 88-89, 115, 140, 151, 169-171

UK (United Kingdom): 112, 114, 132, 139, 144, 153-155

USA: 72, 88, 126

USSR (former): 62, 69, 71-72, 71-83, 90-91, 97, 104

Vatican: 90, 150

Von der Leyen, Ursula: 8, 158, 160, 162-163

Wilhelm of Wied: 35, 47-48

Young Turks: 27-28

Zog (King): 7, 54-57, 64-66, 68, 100, 182